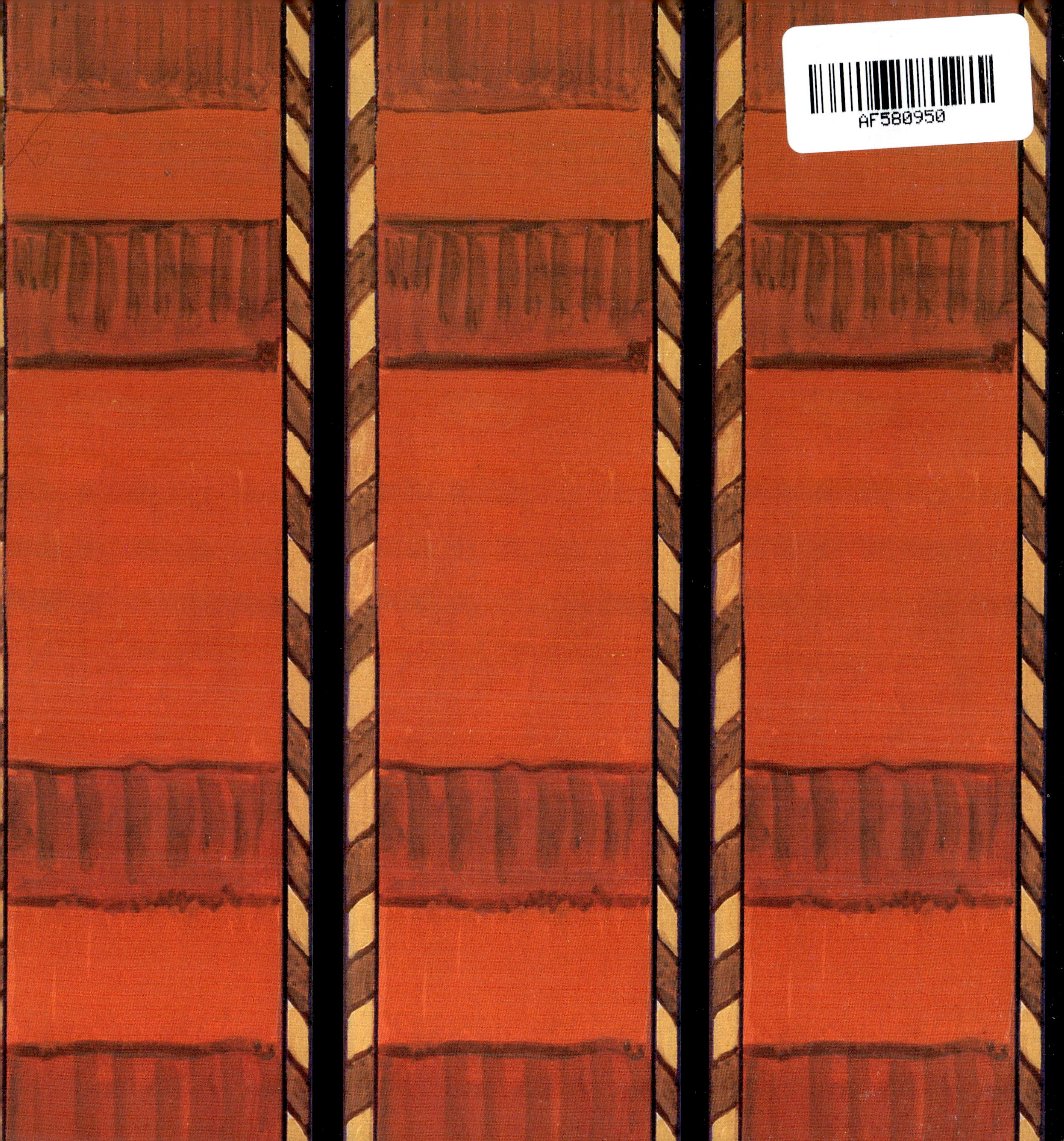

Cover:
Buckeye Blake: Art on the Western Front, 1993.
Gouache on illustration board; 30 x 24 inches.
Loan from the Collection of Buckeye Blake.

Preceding Page:
Buckeye Blake: Art on the Western Front (detail), 1993.

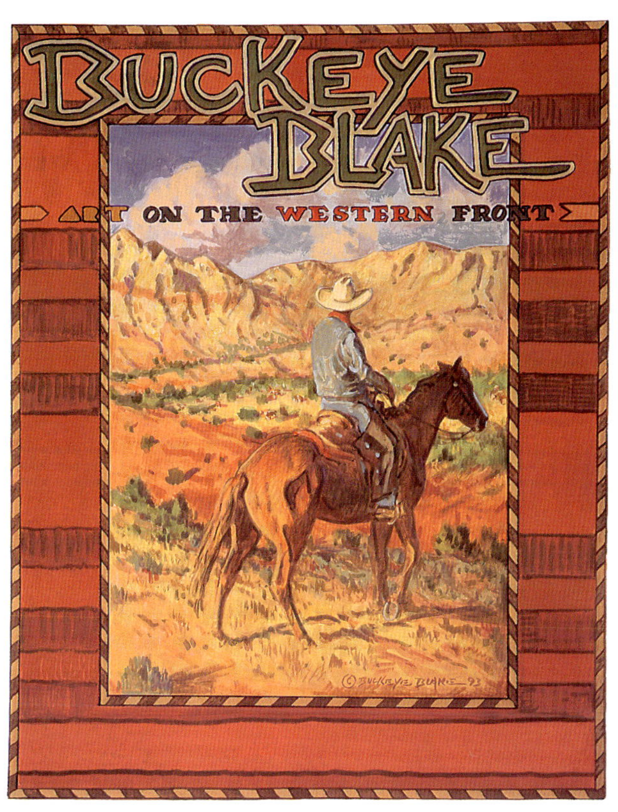

SARAH E. BOEHME

INTRODUCTION BY
THOMAS McGUANE

Published by the Buffalo Bill Historical Center, Cody, Wyoming,
in association with the University of Washington Press, Seattle and London.

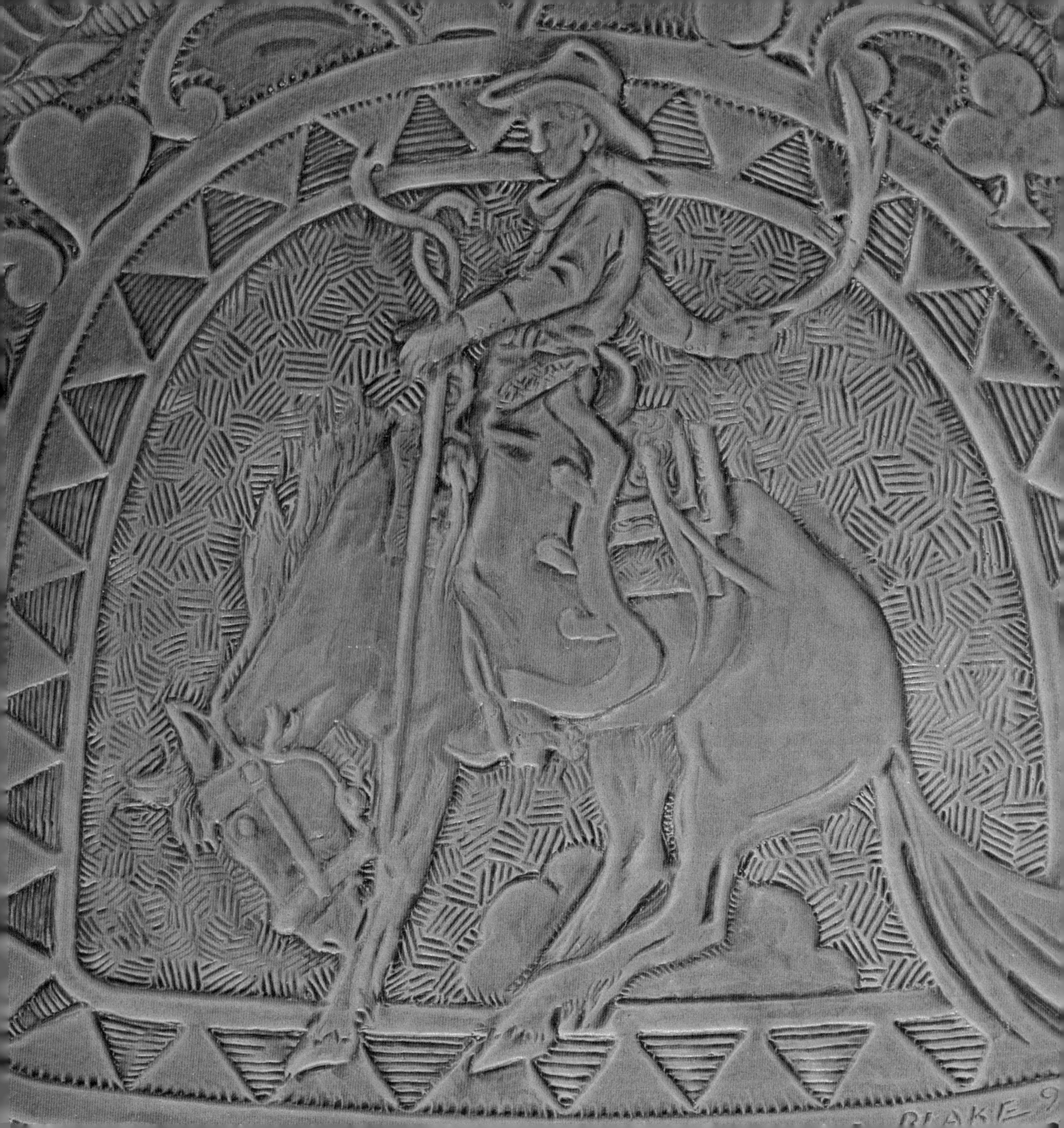
BLAKE

PREFACE

PETER H. HASSRICK
DIRECTOR, BUFFALO BILL HISTORICAL CENTER

In the big picture of American art, that picture framed by the gilded parameters of New York taste and flamboyantly tinted with modern art theory, realistic painting has been recognized for only about 20 years. In the bigger picture of art in America, that art born of impulse and inspiration taken west of the Hudson River, realistic painting has been healthy for much longer. Here, art did not get sidetracked into finding its sole relevance in abstraction and then wrestling itself free of the lessons thus learned. Out in the hinterlands, where figurative traditions have thrived over the three generations of this century, art developed with relative ease and honesty.

In its most refreshing forms, that art found unique expressions that reflected the diversity of cultural adaptations and regional self-identities. In the West, there is no more lively testimonial to regional figurative expression than the art of Buckeye Blake. United with a technique that exudes a kinetic vitality, a compelling wit and an unfettered, whimsical style, Blake's paintings, sculpture and decorative work are transfused with life. As a true son of the West, he is a reflection of regional characteristics, while his art is an equal reflection of Blake the man. He proves that clear thinking, unbounded energy and a good sense of design, added to knowledge and experience of western life ways, can produce an uncommon art form. Sprinkle some creative genius into the formula and Buckeye Blake, a distinctly uncommon artist, emerges.

We would like to thank the many private collectors, museums and galleries who have graciously consented to lend works to *Buckeye Blake: Art on the Western Front.* Their willingness to share Blake's art has made it possible for the museum to present a wide range of exemplary pieces. For helping to reveal the diversity of creative force represented in Blake's work, we owe special thanks and recognition to Sarah E. Boehme, John S. Bugas Curator of the Whitney Gallery of Western Art. Her selection of works and insightful essay afford us a broad understanding of Blake, his subjects and style. We are also grateful to Bob and Nancy Brown of the Big Horn Gallery, Cody, Wyoming, for their generous assistance in helping to organize the exhibition and supporting the show financially. In addition, we are indebted to the Greenwich Workshop, Inc., Trumbull, Connecticut, for helping underwrite the cost of publishing this catalogue as well as the invitation to the exhibition opening and the poster which accompanies the exhibition. The exhibition catalogue has been published in association with the University of Washington Press, Seattle and London. Likewise we owe thanks to Dan W. Lufkin, James G. Taggart, Hannah and Stuart Cutshall, Jim and Sue King, Mr. & Mrs. Philip R. Rulon, and Mantha Phillips. Thanks also are due to Matt Hahn, who designed the catalogue, poster and invitation. Other members of our museum staff who have been especially helpful in bringing this exhibition to fruition include Frances Clymer, curatorial assistant; Wally Reber, assistant director; Dena Hollowell, curatorial secretary; Paul Brock, operating engineer; Paul Rich, cabinet maker; Joanne Kudla, registrar; Elizabeth Holmes, associate registrar; Suzanne G. Tyler, director of publications; Devendra Shrikhande, head photographer; and Lucille Warters, photographer.

Left:
Chair (detail of seat), 1993.
Wood and embossed leather;
29 x 20 x 23 inches.
Loan from Due-West Furniture,
Rindge, New Hampshire.

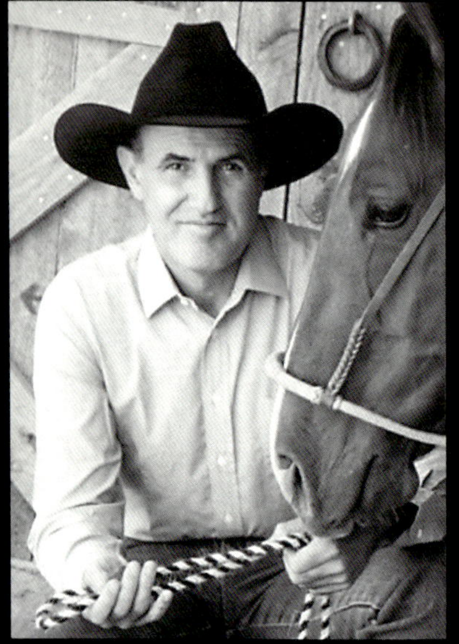

Buckeye Blake, 1993.
Photograph by Tona Freeman Blake.

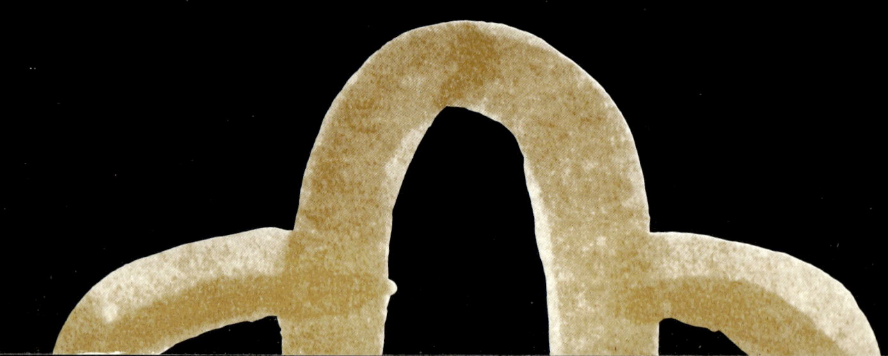

BUCKEYE BLAKE

THOMAS McGUANE

Buckeye Blake is so thorough a westerner that it would never occur to him to mention it. His father was a rodeo cowboy who eventually worked for the Arizona border patrol. His great-grandfather, Coke Blake, was one of the pioneer breeders of quarter horses. Buckeye has lived in Arizona, Nevada and, now, Montana, as well as such thoroughly exotic locales as California and El Salvador. Most of us who live in the West have a similar list of geographical investigations. Its spaces invite the vagabond. To be otherwise indicates a certain paucity of spirit in a region characterized by what the bureaucrats call a "low persistence rate," or chronic turnover. This may say more about the West's inviting horizons than it does its inhabitants' failure to stay in one spot very long. The West still contains sufficient Edenic delights to induce wandering and exploratory forays; yes, even today. The vaunted "permanence" of many Eastern venues implies a lack of curiosity beyond property lines. So, we are stuck with that bureaucratic condemnation, "a low persistence rate."

Blake has his home place now, a pretty house in a small town on the Rocky Mountain Front in Montana, filled with evocative curiosities he and his wife have gathered. His son, fascinated by animals, has his own gathering of creatures, not excluding snakes and lizards, which are the normal appurtenances of this sort of house. There is a stable in back where, among several well cared-for horses, is the blue roan Blake rides to work a few miles away. He paints in a small building on the edge of a shapely prairie which, at evening light, seems, and probably is, filled with ghosts. Here he works through various weathers and seasons, throwing open windows or stoking the wood stove.

I have also seen Blake in a rented cinderblock house on the edge of Tucson, the vestiges of a rural settlement crumbling into haphazard suburbia, a house full of an absentee owner's furniture, his easel set up in a low ceilinged vacant room with bad light. He was doing just fine there too. In this vulgar place, something bright and visionary and original was lighting up on the canvas, a perimeter of raw white fabric yielding to the expanding paint and the pressing ideas.

At cutting horse contests, Blake has let me look at paintings he was hauling in his horse trailer. For a while we had several heroic-size paintings of migrant workers with a sense of eternity captured in their forms and faces, stored in our barn pending shipment to their new owner in California.

With a real lack of preciosity or self-consciousness, Blake has turned to notional small paintings, some crossing into the forbidden Valley of the Anecdote with singular high spirits, rodeo posters, illustrations, bookmarks, triptychs, friezes, all in the vigor that separates artists from careerists. Speeding beneath the surface of much of his life and work is a fascinating, almost ungraspable, sense of comedy as well as a distinctive ironic tension.

Once, in Roundup, Montana, Blake and I were staying across the hall from one another in an old motel. It was summertime and the air conditioners had failed. Rather than try to repair them, the owner had torn them from the walls leaving gaping holes that stared into the street below. We had put our horses up at the lovely old fairgrounds along the Musselshell River. Blake took me to see an old house in a sidestreet we reached by a back alley strewn with the nodding heads of huge sunflowers. The house was a weathered derelict, a tall narrow thing whose owner had decorated nearly every inch of it with signs of the zodiac, bursts of arbitrary color, bumper stickers, biblical enjoinders, outlandish political statements and animal heads. It was hard to take it all in. Beyond the end of the crumbling street, I could make out the rimrock and pine breaks of open country. The blue sky of Montana was overhead.

Buckeye Blake looked happy.

BUCKEYE BLAKE

ART ON THE WESTERN FRONT

SARAH E. BOEHME

The art of Buckeye Blake belongs firmly and self-consciously to an American tradition of "cowboy art." While securely rooted in this heritage, Blake's art also belongs to a new western artistic front which engages the past with a modern sensibility, and which knows that art can wear several different hats, from Stetson to sunbonnet. The American West has generated an art defined by an iconography of the region, realized with stylistic variations circumscribed by a fidelity to nature, and based on an implicit theoretical foundation which espouses experience as the guarantee of authenticity and therefore of value. In other words, cowboy art shows scenes of cowboys, pictured realistically, and made by real cowboys who know their subject because they have lived it. Buckeye paints and sculpts ten-gallon-hatted, bowlegged, bronc-busting cowboys in a lifelike way, and he has the genuine horseback experiences to back it up. But in his awareness that he is making art, Blake also finds the freedom to stylize his realism, to smile sometimes when portraying the hero, and to portray the West with a larger cast of players. His art resolutely faces its identity, rather than only looking backward (cover).

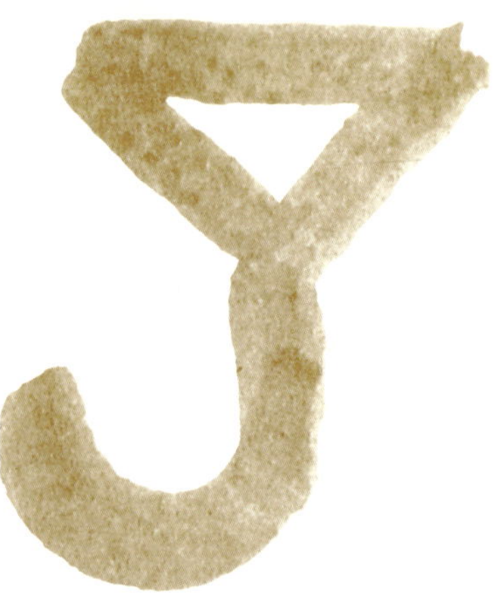

As a contemporary western artist, Blake is grounded in the tradition of the artist who has learned his craft by learning his subject. Within the history of American art there has always been a pragmatic element; artistic work has often had a functional role, such as communicating information or documenting history. The artist who knows his subject has an advantage. In western art, this pragmatism has resulted in a privileged position for the cowboy-artist, whose life on the range has given him the knowledge and experience to represent accurately and with personal firsthand insight the subjects of western life.

For Blake and for other of this century's legion of western artists, the classic artists who serve as exemplars of this tradition were Frederic Remington (Plate 1) and Charles M. Russell (Plate 2). Remington, although never a working cowboy, traveled in the West, rode horseback in the western territories, and as an outdoorsman experienced the region's characteristics. He studied the particularities of the landscape, the clothing and the gear of the West. His knowledge informed his paintings and sculptures and convinced his eastern audience of their authenticity. Remington's talents and skills as an artist serve as an inspiration for contemporary artists such as Blake, who finds—especially in Remington's late works—a sense of the essence of the West.

Yet whatever claims Remington might have as a purveyor of the genuine article, he is eclipsed by Charles M. Russell, who lived most of his life in Montana. Russell worked as a wrangler and knew the cowboy's gear not only from studio study but primarily from everyday use. Self-taught in art, he exemplified the American independent spirit and a western pride in freedom from academic influence. Russell is more likely to be cited by westerners as the true Cowboy Artist. Blake has paid tribute to Russell at key points in his career. The first bronze sculpture that Blake ever produced, *Rainbow Trail*, 1980, portrayed Russell's funeral cortege. In collaboration with Gil Melton who made the coach, Blake used photographs and research to design the scene of horsedrawn hearse, outriders, and riderless horse to signify the departed.

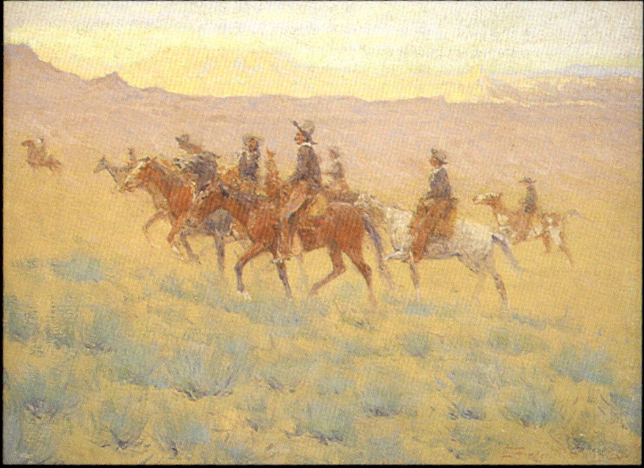

Plate 1:
Frederic S. Remington,
Ghosts of the Past, ca. 1908.
Oil on canvas; 12 x 16 inches.
Buffalo Bill Historical Center, Cody, Wyoming.
Gift of The Coe Foundation.

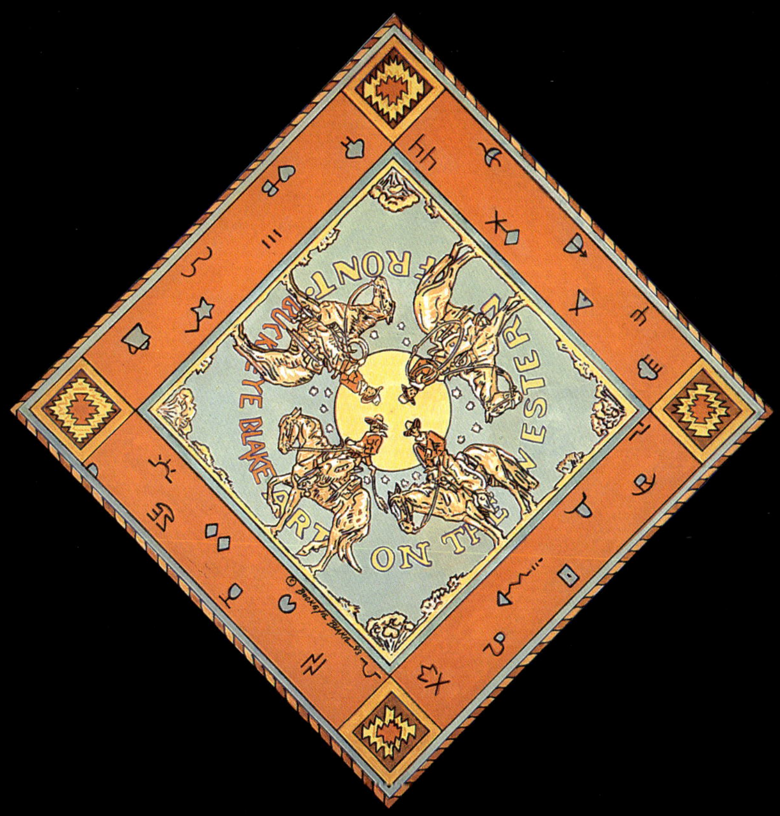

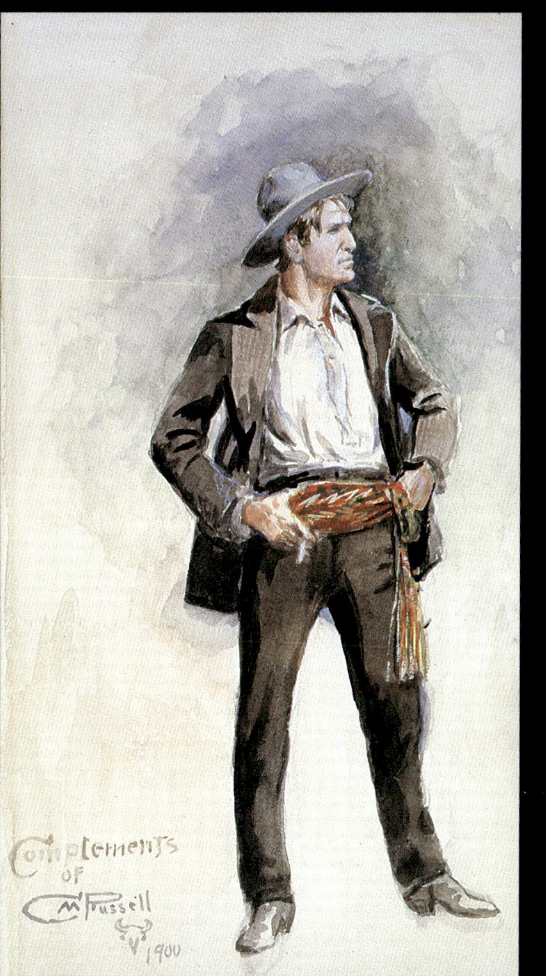

Plate 2:
Charles Marion Russell,
Self Portrait, 1900.
Watercolor on paper; 12 5/8 x 7 1/8 inches.
Buffalo Bill Historical Center, Cody, Wyoming.
Gift of Charles Ulrick and Josephine Bay Foundation, Inc.

Plate 3:
Buckeye Blake: Art on the Western Front, Bandana Design, 1993.
Gouache on illustration board;
20 1/8 x 20 1/8 inches.
Loan from the Collection of Buckeye Blake.

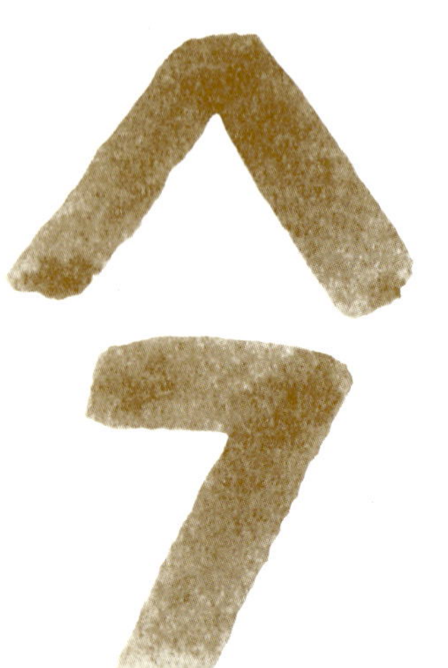

Artistically Blake surpassed this early homage with a major work in his career, the monumental *Kid Russell and Monte, Circa 1889,* 1986, which stands in downtown Great Falls, Montana. The smaller version of the sculpture (Plate 4) repeats the composition of the monument and adds the element of color. Appropriately inspired by the famous artist, Blake sought to represent Russell authentically by making certain that the details were correct. He modeled the saddle on one of Russell's at the Montana Historical Society; he based Russell's clothing on known examples and the artist's self portraits. He studied not only Russell's history, but also, importantly for this work, the biography of his horse. Beyond the accumulation of accurate details, Blake portrays the legendary artist in an original conception. Blake's sculpture portrays Russell *with*, but significantly, not *on*, his horse Monte. His hat pushed back in a characteristic fashion, Russell stands in a relaxed contrapposto pose, with one arm encircling Monte. The cayuse turns his head back to communicate with his caretaker. The informal grace of this composition is in stark contrast to most representations of man and horse. Equestrian sculptures with mounted figures have traditionally been a sign of royalty or power. Blake chose to portray Russell in a moment of equality with his beloved equine companion. The depiction emphasizes the importance of the horse in western art and western life, and specifically portrays Russell as the sympathetic lover of animals. By coloring the smaller version, Blake signals another influence from Russell. Connoisseurs of Russell's art cherish the painted wax sculptures which Russell fashioned for friends and family. Although Russell did not paint his bronzes, he sometimes made plaster casts, which he did paint. The application of color to bronzes has become an important stylistic development in western art, revived by artist Harry Jackson. Blake's use of applied color on *Kid Russell and Monte* serves to heighten the realism of the depiction and to highlight significant details such as the red voyageur sash.

Buckeye Blake has the background and experience to qualify as a contemporary cowboy. His great-grandfather S. Coke Blake, of Pryor, Oklahoma, was one of the foundation breeders of quarter horses in the early 20th century. From his parents he received influences affecting both portions of the cowboy artist equation. His father, Bud, was a rodeo rider; his mother, Dee, was an artist. Born in 1946 in Fullerton, California, James Coke Blake quickly felt the effect of rodeo life.

Plate 4:
Kid Russell and Monte, Circa 1889, 1986.
Bronze, polychromed;
18 1/2 x 20 1/2 x 13 1/2 inches.
Number 24 of an edition of 26.
Loan courtesy Big Horn Gallery,
Cody, Wyoming.

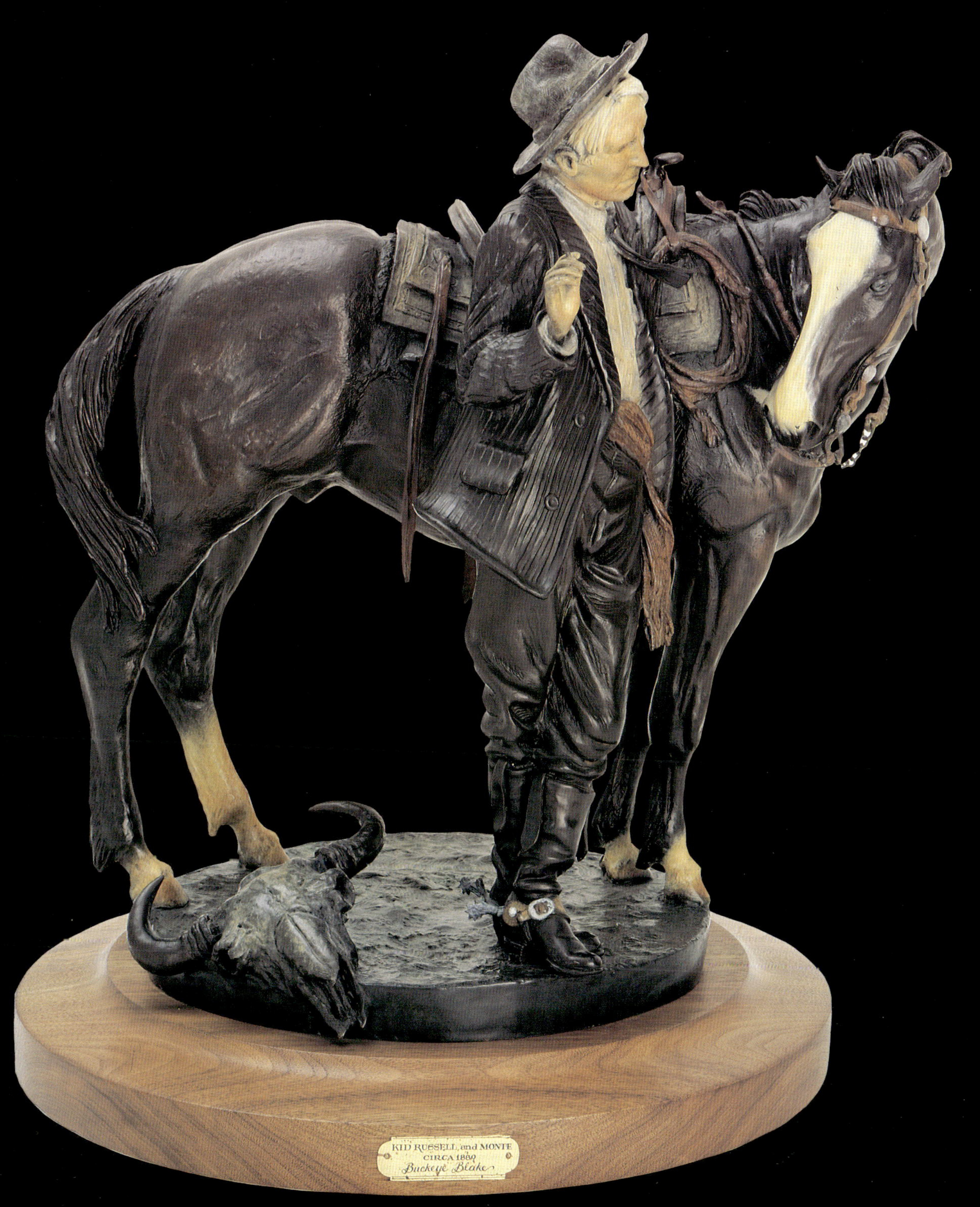
KID RUSSELL and MONTE
CIRCA 1889
Buckeye Blake

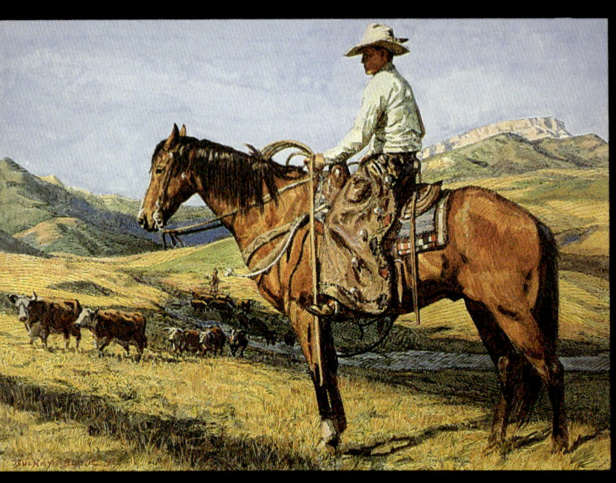

Plate 5:
His Grandfather's Chaps, 1992.
Gouache, pen and ink on illustration board; 20 x 28 inches.
Loan from James G. Taggart, Cody, Wyoming.

The nickname by which he is known came from the rodeo town of Buckeye, Arizona, through which the family passed as the future artist was beginning to speak. By calling himself Buckeye, he fashioned his own western name. Blake's watercolor of a young cowboy *His Grandfather's Chaps,* 1992 (Plate 5) was a commission for a patron, yet it can also serve as a reminder of Blake's own heritage. In the painting, the chaps with the painted-on emblems of the family's brand symbolize the passing of western traditions from generation to generation.

Growing up traveling on the rodeo circuit, Buckeye saw western life that had already begun to reflect on its past. The rodeo itself transformed the traditional skills of horsemanship and livestock management needed by the everyday cowboy into a sport-performance and competition. After moving around the West for rodeos and other occupations, the family eventually settled on a ranch outside Carson City, Nevada. Buckeye Blake himself abstained from the rodeo arena, and instead has chosen to ride in cutting horse competition. Like rodeo, the cutting horse competition takes a traditional skill and transforms it into a competitive sport performed for an audience. However, riding a cutting horse is different from most rodeo events. Instead of pitting the rider against the horse as in bucking horse events, the cutting horse competition demands coordination of rider and mount, precision, skill and timing. These qualities find parallels in Blake's approach to art. He has made the cutting horse part of his iconography, as in the painting *The Cutting Edge,* 1991 (Plate 6). He has expressed the close relationship between rider and horse in works such as *Kid Russell and Monte,* and he approaches his subjects with grace and skill.

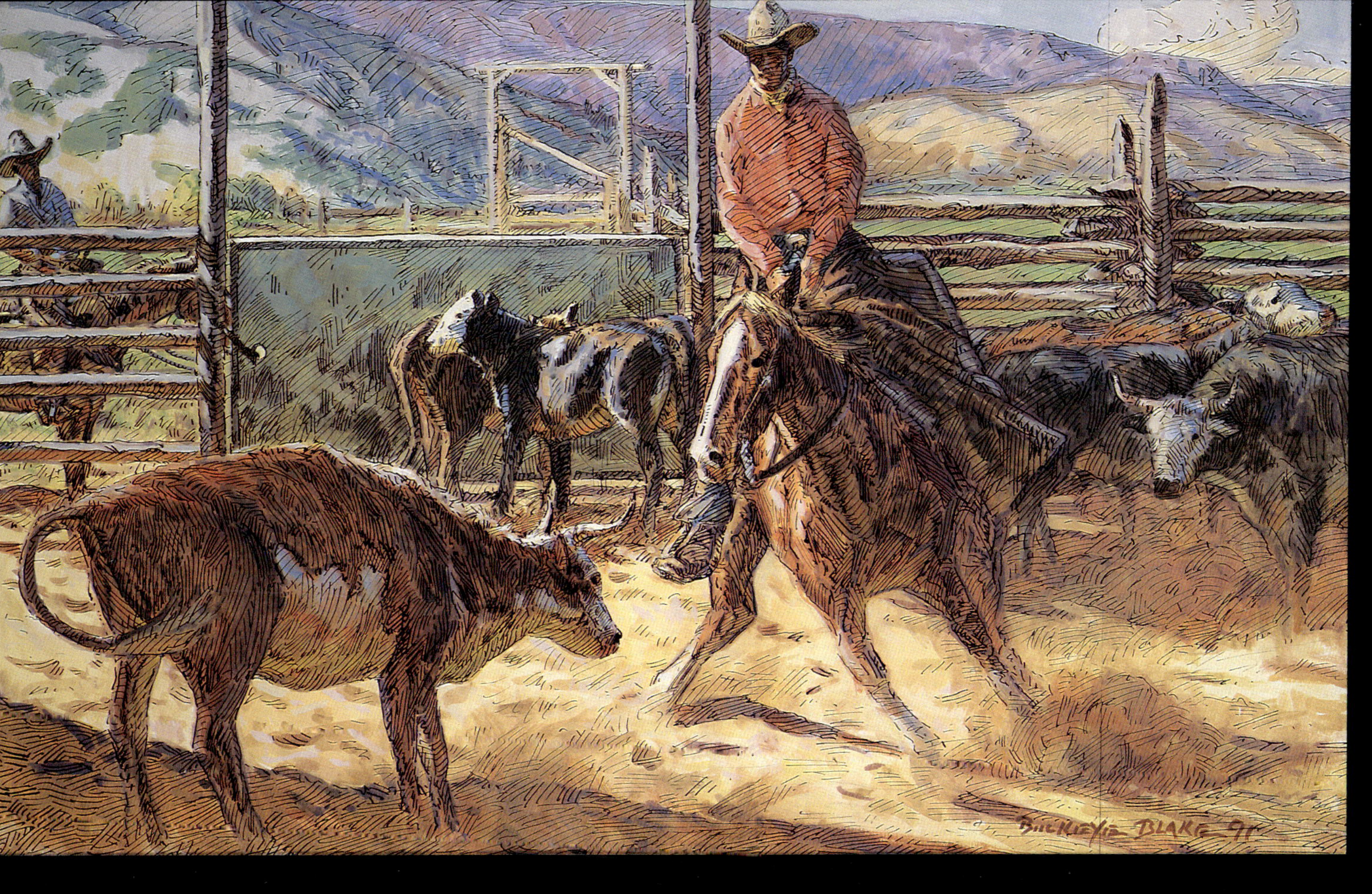

Plate 6:
The Cutting Edge, 1991.
Gouache, pen and ink on illustration board; $19\,^{15}/_{16}$ x 30 inches.
Loan from Mr. and Mrs. Phil Redman, Billings, Montana.

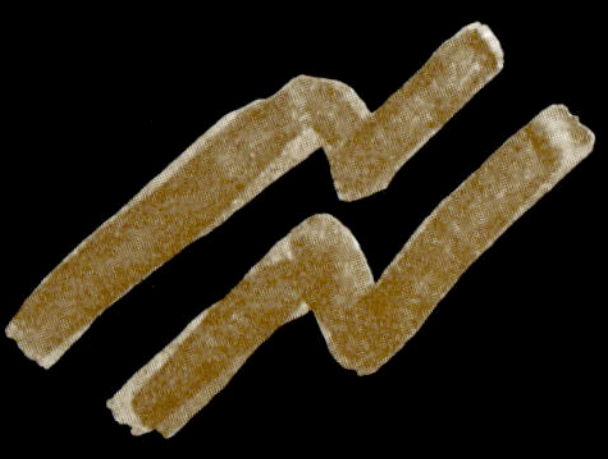

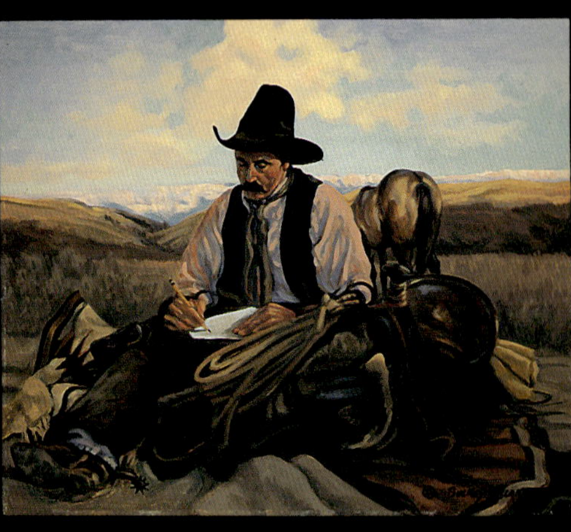

Plate 7:
Writing Home, 1984.
Oil on board; 20 x 24 1/8 inches.
Loan from Sam and Denise Abell.

Blake has also chosen the rural life of the West. He left Nevada when he was 17 to go to Hollywood, California, where he worked for some studios painting scenery. Missing the sagebrush, he soon moved back to Nevada, working construction and ranch jobs to support himself while doing art on the side. Like his predecessor Russell, Blake eventually decided to work fulltime as an artist. He made his commitment at about the same time as he made a move to Charlie Russell country in 1978. Feeling that Nevada had become too industrial, Buckeye and his wife Tona Freeman Blake settled in the small town of Augusta, Montana, about an hour from Great Falls, where Russell spent most of his career. Nestled against the Front Range of the Montana Rockies, Augusta provides solitude, a connection with landscape, and the space to raise a few horses. Blake's current studio, outside the town, was formerly a livery stable which he moved to the site. Blake has also spent winters in Arizona, where the southwestern desert, the culture of the Navajo and other tribes of the region, and the Spanish heritage provide rich sources of inspiration for a western artist, and the proximity of other artists and writers provides a broader cultural context. Yet for Blake the setting of Montana and its seclusion produced the best conditions for making his art.

Blake's own experiences and identity make the cowboy and his work the dominant theme in his artistic work, and he dramatically declares that in works such as *Cowboy*, 1990 (Plate 8). The painting *Writing Home*, 1984 (Plate 7) depicts a cowboy sitting cross-legged on the blanketed ground, putting pencil to paper. In his high-crowned hat the cowboy, sitting with one leg outstretched and his saddle as an armrest, forms a triangular shape which anchors the composition. His unsaddled horse blends with the tawny colors of the background. Linked with its title, the painting tells a story of a solitary cowboy who takes a break from his work to write a letter back home. The painting is also a self-portrait, and seen in that genre, it presents the essence of the cowboy-artist. The pencil and paper portray the artistic process as the elements of cowboy life support the work. The cowboy is literally down-to-earth with the open prairie, distant mountains and big sky serving as a studio. *Writing Home* also represents a turning point in Blake's career. Early works in Blake's career featured a linear style with broadly drawn figures, reminiscent of cartoon style characters. In the early 1980s, as Blake produced more paintings, his work took a more serious tone. In this painting he used a crisp outline to delineate the figure, but nevertheless gracefully modeled his forms.

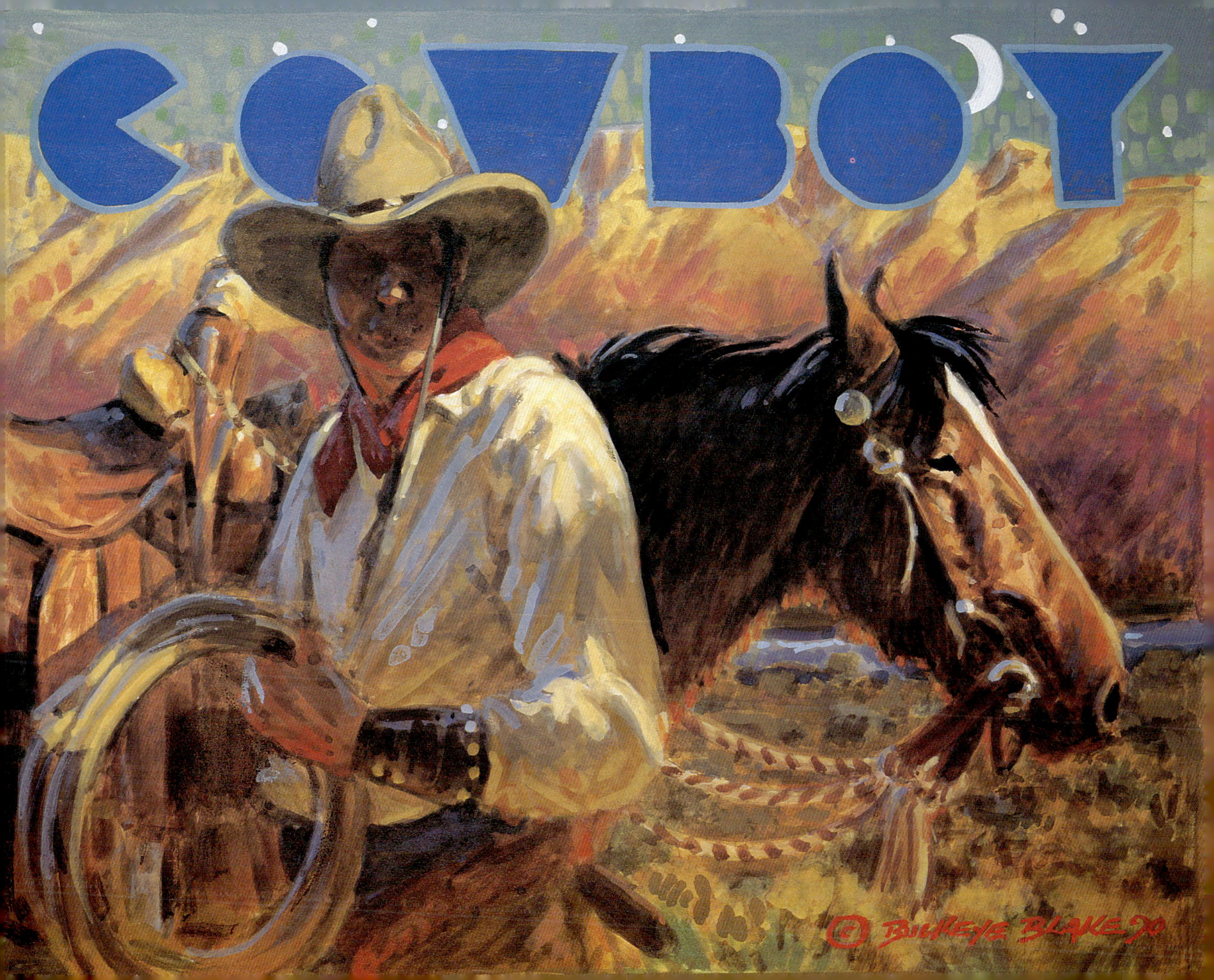
COWBOY
© BUCKEYE BLAKE '90

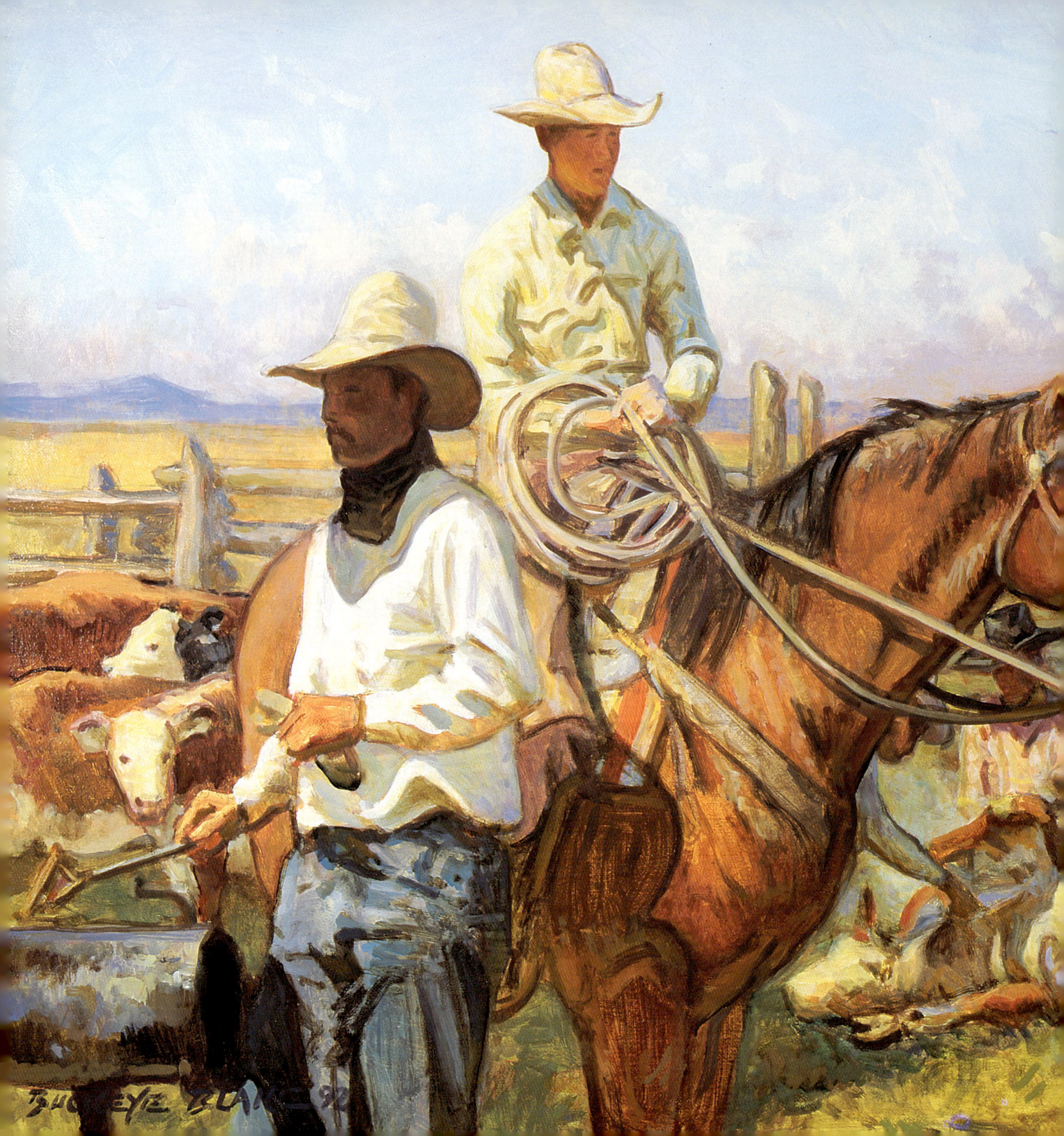

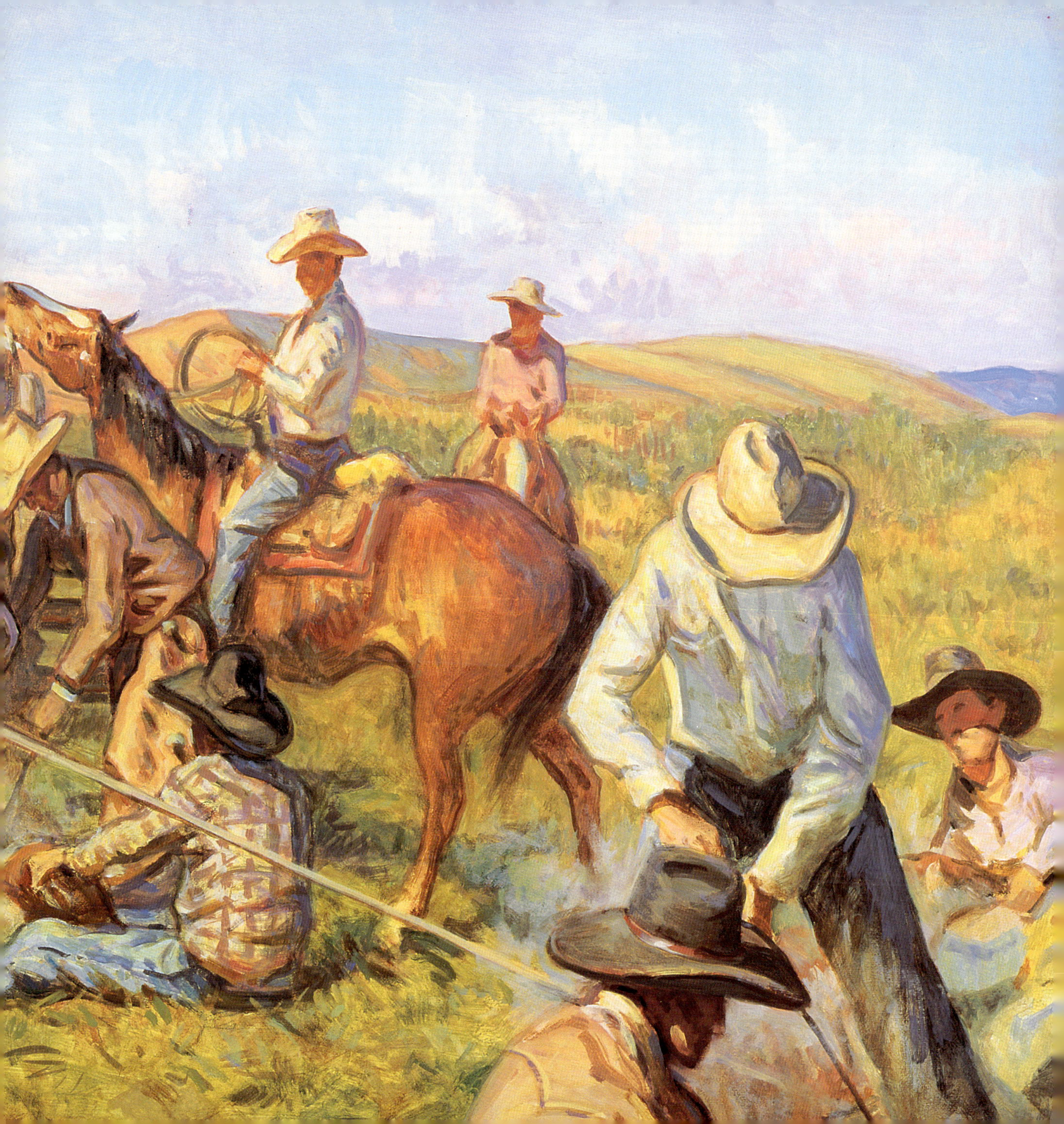

Preceding Page
Plate 9:
A Cowboy's Work, 1992.
Oil on canvas; 24 x 48 1/4 inches.
Loan from Tom and Laurie McGuane.

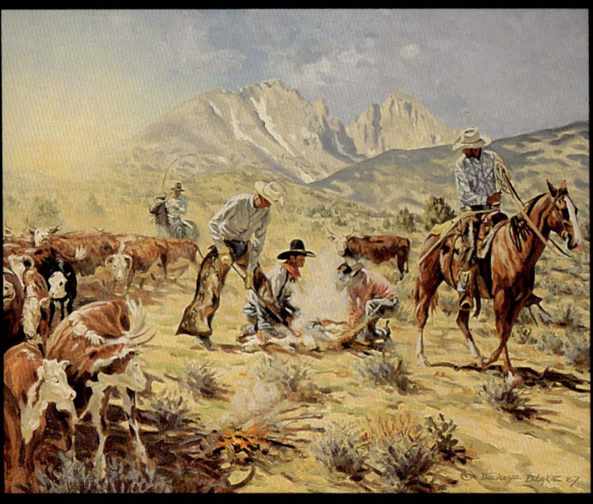

Plate 10:
East of Ely, 1987.
Oil on board; 24 x 30 inches.
Loan from the Collection of Robert Bartlett.

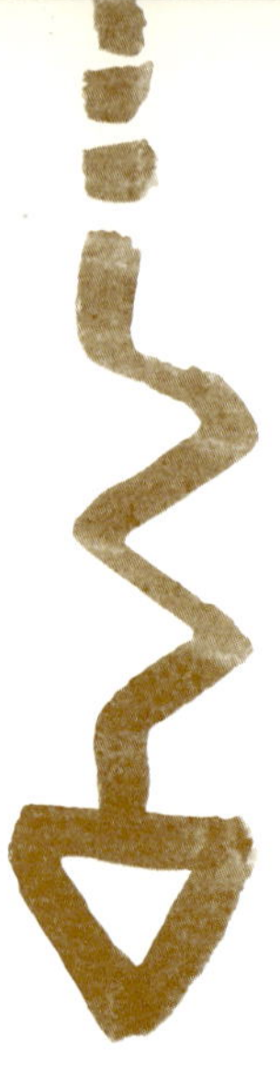

Everyday life on the ranch, the dignity of work in the outdoors, is a focal point in Blake's art. In a painting composition suggesting a relief, with parallel planes of action diminishing in depth, *A Cowboy's Work,* 1992 (Plate 9, preceding page) delineates the multiple tasks of ranch work. In the painting *East of Ely,* 1987 (Plate10), the work focuses on a branding, one of the tasks of cattle management with a long history in the West. The branding occupies the center of the composition. On the left the cattle herd forms a semi-circle framing the scene. The pose of the cowboy with the branding iron echoes the shape of the cattle herd. His iron and the taut rope from the calf's leg to the saddle horn of the roper form a V-shape, leading the eye to the calf. The foreground of sagebrush plain and the background of sharp, glacier-streaked mountains form a solemn space for the action.

The Critics, 1991 (Plate 11) portrays a calf roper whose work is being evaluated by a fence-leaning row of reviewers. The title may be an ironic reference to art critics as well. Roping is a favorite subject of Blake's, and he makes the roper an heroic figure in many paintings. According to Blake, "Roping is a way of understanding the laws of nature." The way that the roper throws his rope has specific consequences; the roper intuitively learns laws of physics through his actions. Throwing the lasso is also akin to art, in that the rope makes a line, and it is pleasing to the eye to watch the arc. The rope in *A Cowboy's Work* unites the composition and with its taut diagonal adds an element of controlled tension. Blake shares with C.M. Russell an interest in roping scenes; in the cowboy's handling of the rope the artists find the beauty of line.

Right
Plate 11:
The Critics, 1991.
Gouache, pen and ink on illustration board; 15 1/2 x 24 inches.
Loan from the Private Collection of Jay L. Reedy.

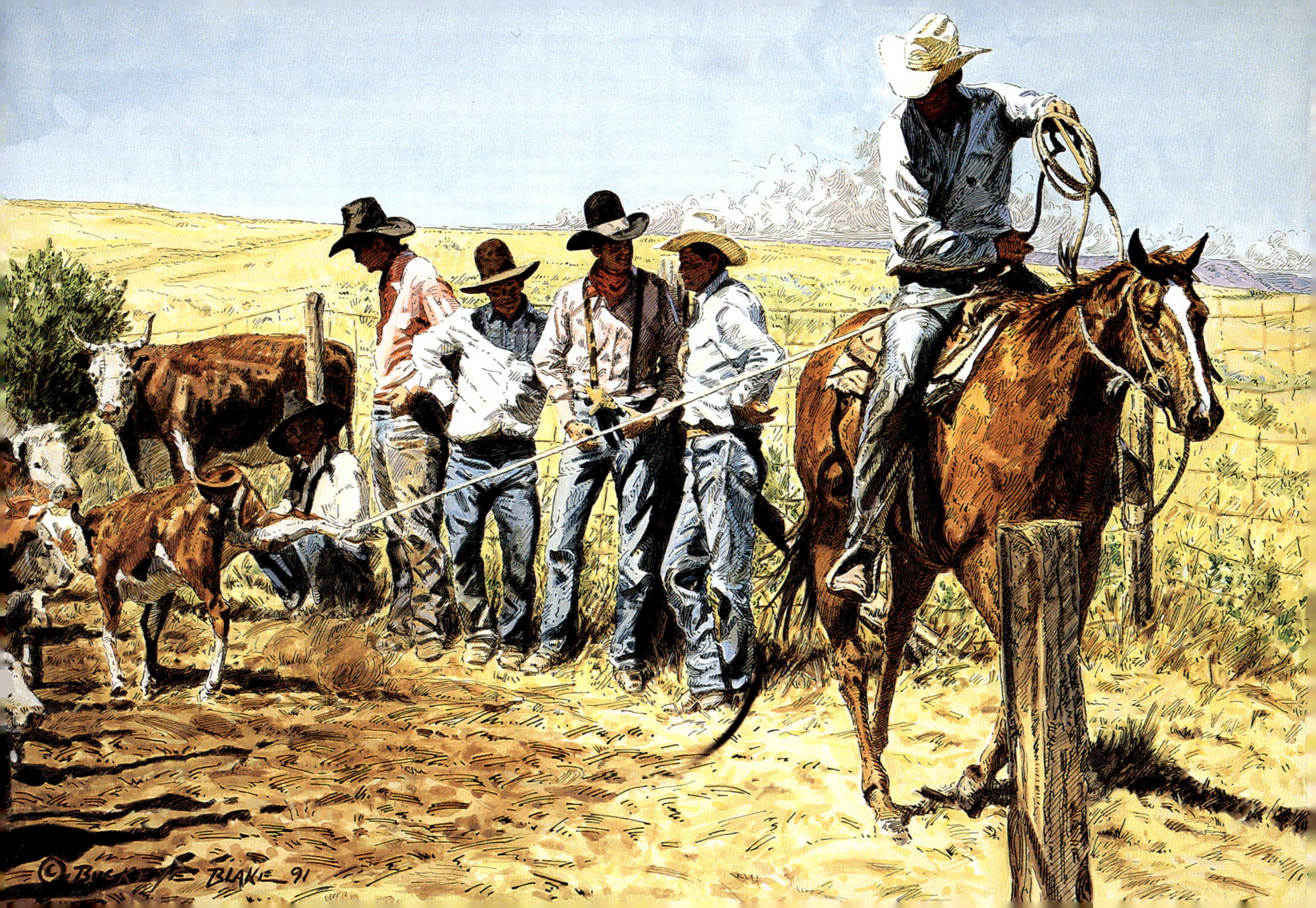
© BUCKEYE BLAKE '91

Right
Plate 13:
The Outlaw Dobie Gray, 1989.
Oil on canvas; 48 7/16 x 60 3/16 inches.
Loan from Mr. and Mrs. Robert L. Noland.

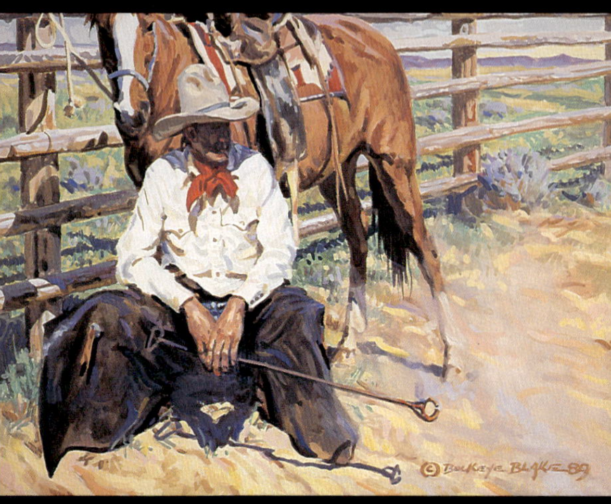

Plate 12:
The Broken O, 1989.
Gouache on paper; 12 x 15 5/16 inches.
Buffalo Bill Historical Center, Cody, Wyoming.
William E. Weiss Purchase Award,
Buffalo Bill Art Show 1989.

Blake's subjects are drawn from the ranchers and workers he knows in his life in the West. *The Broken O,* 1989 (Plate 12) portrays a cowboy from the ranch of that name outside of Augusta. *The Outlaw Dobie Gray,* 1989 (Plate 13) presents the bucking horse theme which is such an important iconographical subject in western art, not as the isolated event of man against wild animal, but within the context of the workings of a ranch. A corral fence parallels the picture plane with two horses and cowboys against it. The outlaw horse, one whose nature resists the imposition of saddle and rider, has thrown the rider. Dobie Gray leaps violently on a diagonal which breaks into the structured plane of the composition. Danger is evident, but appears to be controlled by the cowboy in the highest point of the composition.

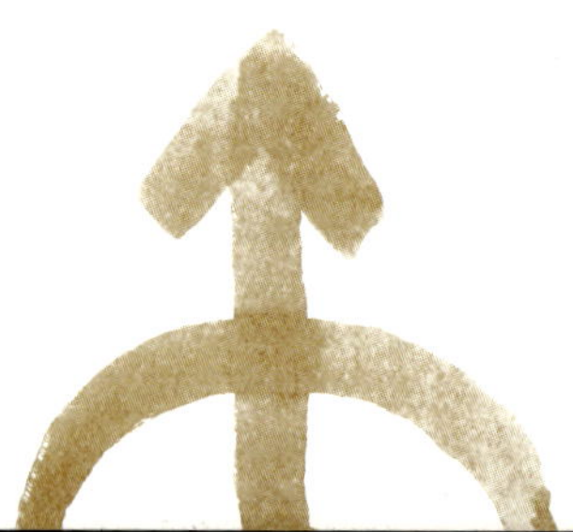

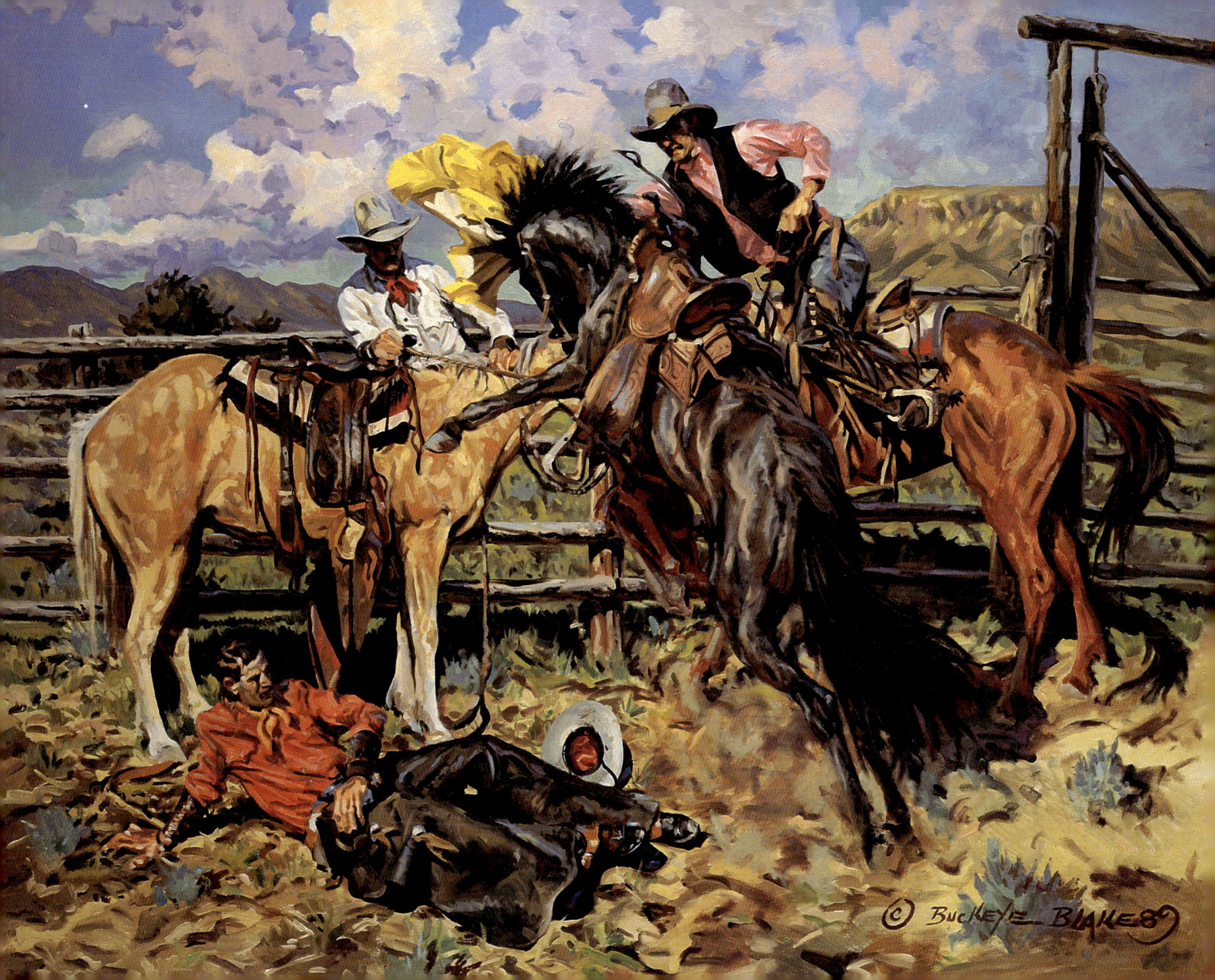
© BUCKEYE BLAKE 89

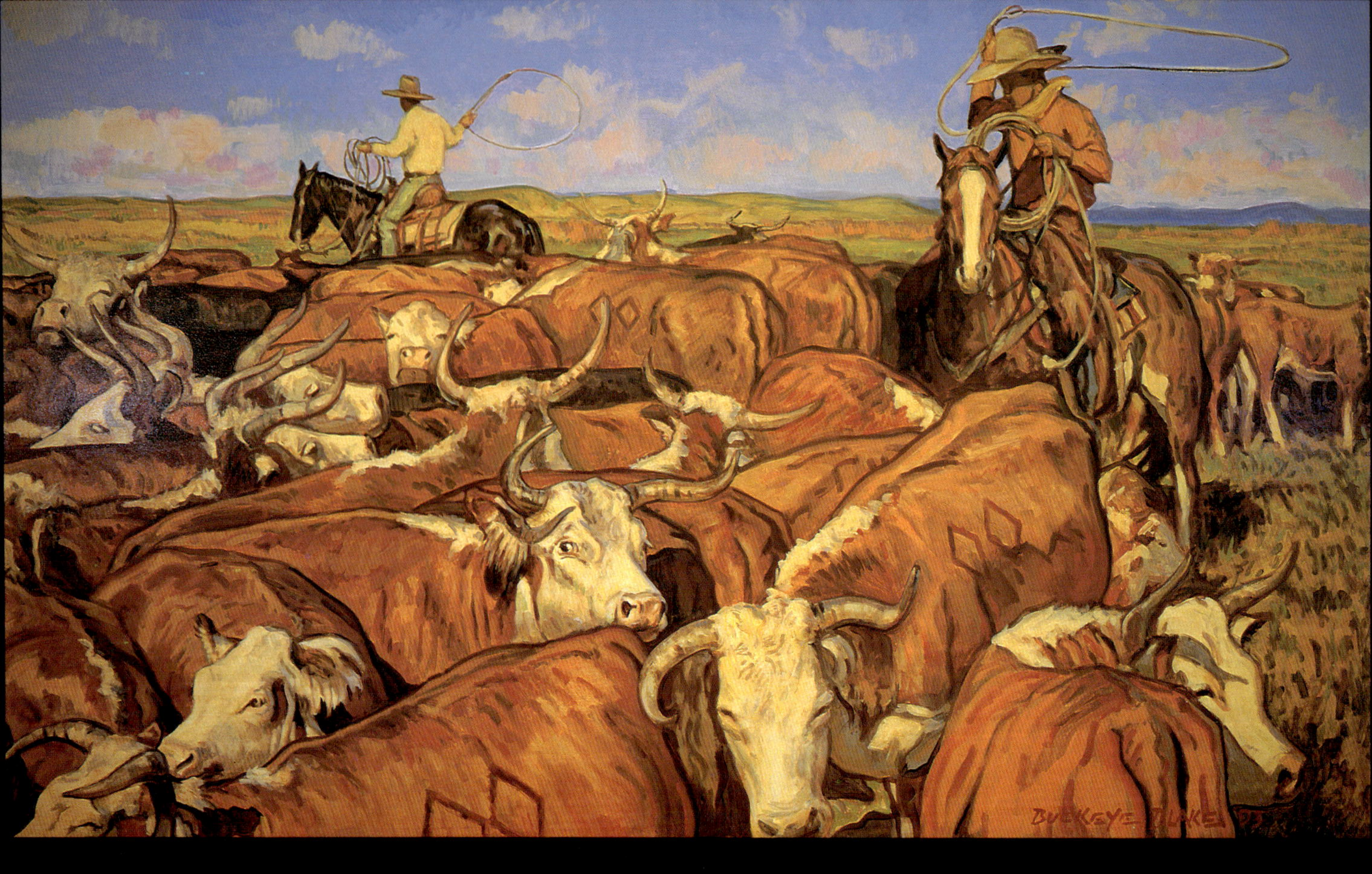

Plate 14:
The Old Double Diamond, 1993.
Oil on canvas; 36 x 60 inches.
Loan from Hannah and Stuart Cutshall.

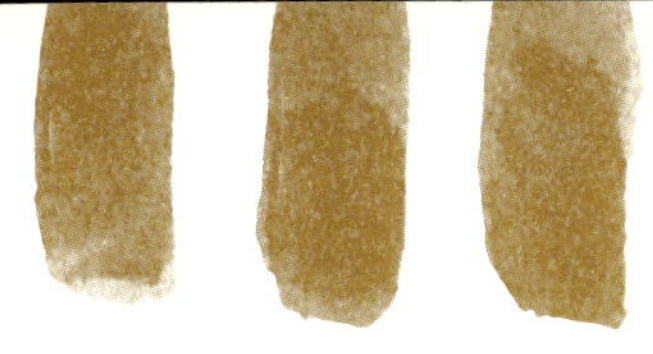

In the recent painting *The Old Double Diamond,* 1993 (Plate 14) Blake shows a real working ranch scene, with cowboys herding range cattle, yet he also evokes the fictional West and the historic West. The title was inspired by the contemporary western ballad by Gary McMahan, *The Old Double Diamond,* a song about a cowboy who looks back at his youth during the sale of one of Wyoming's most historic ranches. Blake's evocation of the song points to the larger cultural context, rich with new music, literature and design, in which the western artist exists. Western music, like western art, draws upon its past and has a strong narrative content rooted in the life of the cowboy, yet in its best manifestations produces original creations with a contemporary sensibility.

Like C.M. Russell and many other American artists, Buckeye Blake is essentially self-taught. This independence from traditional art schools was a product of necessity in the early years in this country when there were few art academies. By the end of the 19th century when Russell painted, there were schools to attend, but the strictures of the academic approach were unappealing to the self-reliant artist. By the time that Blake appeared, the academies were moving in another direction—non-objective art—that would seem superfluous to the young artist attuned to the appearances of the world around him.

Although Blake did not attend formal art school, he has taken workshops from artists such as Ned Jacob, Sergei Bongart and Donald Putman. Equally important, he looks carefully at the works of other artists for inspiration and to learn composition and color. The technology of the modern world—the telephone, rapid travel, printed illustrations—makes it possible for Blake to choose the solitude of Montana and yet remain connected with a larger artistic community. He experiments with different media, often doing multiple versions of a scene in oil, watercolor and pen and ink. His combination of knowledge about the West and knowledge of western artists has led him to paint not only from nature, but also with a consciousness of past styles, especially of western artists. His use of pen and ink with watercolor in works such as *Cowboy on Horse,* 1988 (Plate 15) shows an affinity with the pen and ink style of Charles Russell. The parallel pen strokes in the sky also give the impression of a wood engraving.

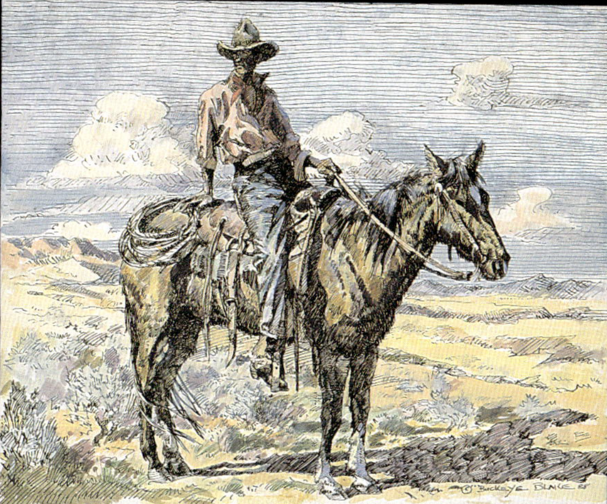

Plate 15:
Cowboy on Horse, 1988.
Watercolor, pen and ink on illustration board; 8 x 10 inches.
Loan from William and Barbara B. Cowan.

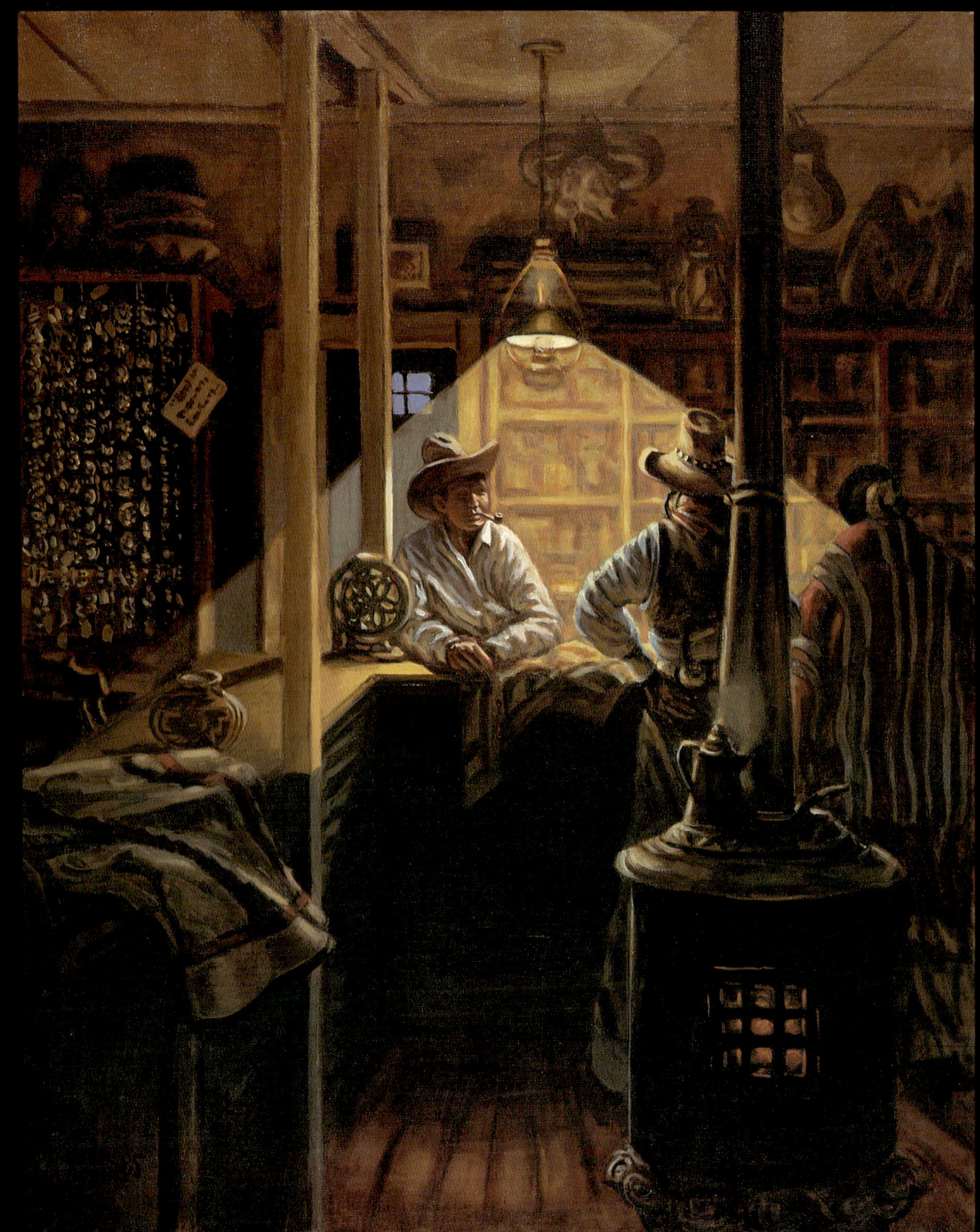

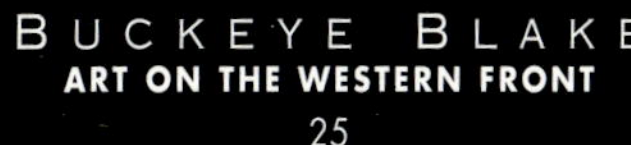

Many of Blake's works which feature the use of pen and ink with watercolor have an old-fashioned appearance because they evoke delicately hand-colored engravings.

He has also looked carefully at western illustrators and has done some work specifically as illustration for printed text. For Philip Reed Rulon's editing of *Navajo Trader,* the autobiography of Gladwell "Tony" Richardson, Blake painted the cover image, *Navajo Trader,* 1985 (Plate 16). In the interior scene of Tony Richardson at the Inscription House trading post, Blake investigates the effects of light and the use of perspective. His modeling of forms with soft contours establishes a link with the Taos artists of the early 20th-century southwest.

Like both Remington and Russell, Blake has pursued his artistic representation of the cowboy in three-dimensional as well as two-dimensional works. His early sculpture of *Rough String Rider,* 1983 (Plate 17) presents the cowboy in a non-heroic pose, seated on the ground.

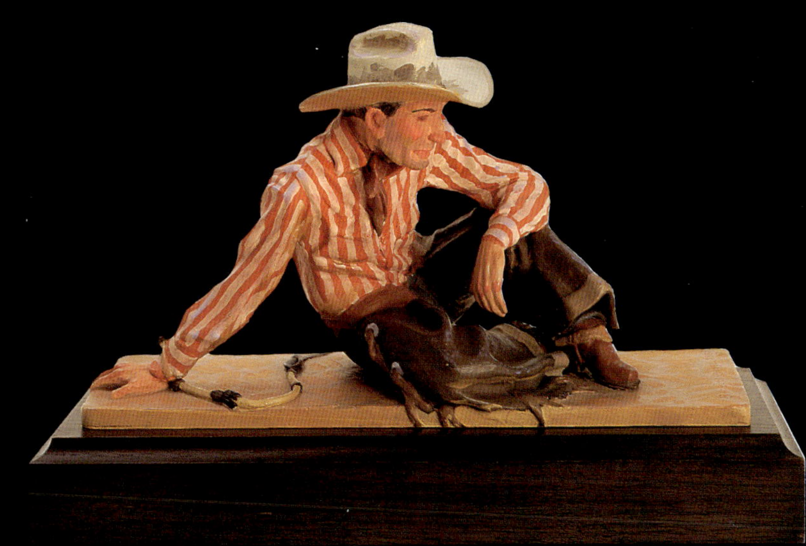

Left
Plate 16:
Navajo Trader, 1985.
Oil on canvas; 30 x 24 inches.
Loan from the Private Collection of Annette K. and Philip Reed Rulon.

Plate 17:
Rough String Rider, 1983.
Bronze, painted; 6 3/4 x 11 1/2 x 6 inch
Artist's Copy.
Loan from Eugene W. Reber.

Right
Plate 19:
Palomino Moon, 1990.
Watercolor, pen and ink
on illustration board;
18 5/8 x 14 1/2 inches.
Loan from Hannah and Stuart Cutshall.

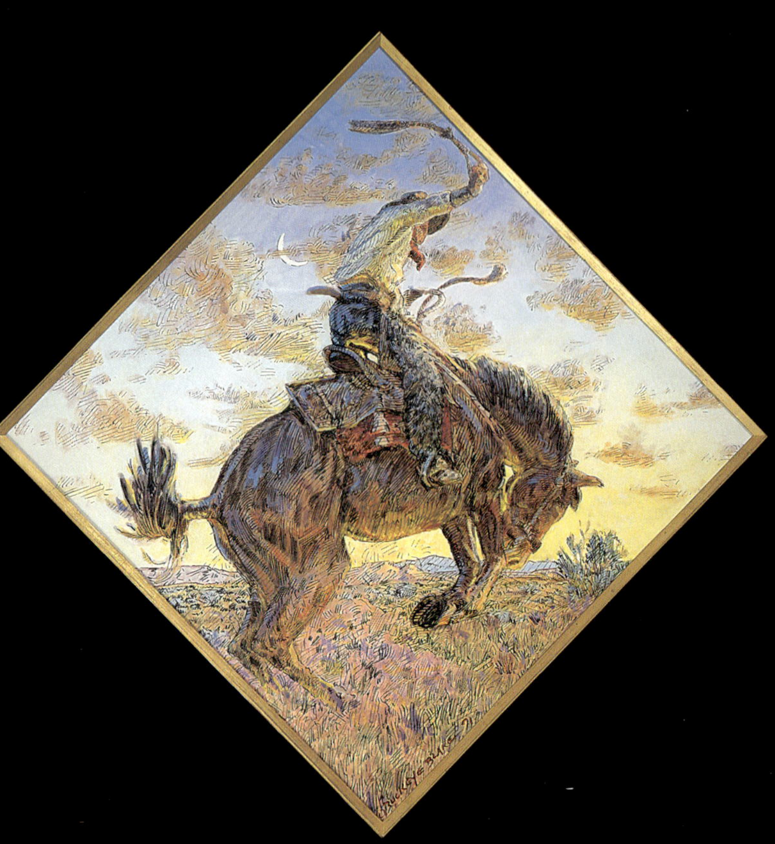

Plate 18:
Showing Daylight, 1991.
Gouache, pen and ink on illustration board; 28 5/16 x 28 5/16 inches.
Loan from Barbara and Jim Schmitt, Jackson, Wyoming.

Blake can also take a romantic view of the cowboy. The traditional western subject of the bucking horse and rider takes on a nostalgic glow in works such as *Showing Daylight,* 1991 (Plate 18). *Palomino Moon,* 1990 (Plate 19) depicts a cowboy who could be out of a movie set. He mounts his golden palomino horse against a flat backdrop of corral fence, mountain range and black sky dotted with golden stars. Blake embellished the mat with brands, graphic symbols of the cowboy's history. Brands appear as graphic elements in many of his works, serving as decorative elements, as signs of the West's history, and as evidence of visual symbolism in the western tradition.

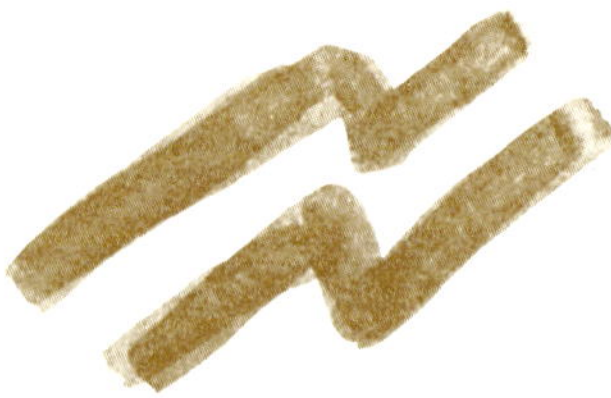

III W 44

© Buckeye Blake 90

XIT

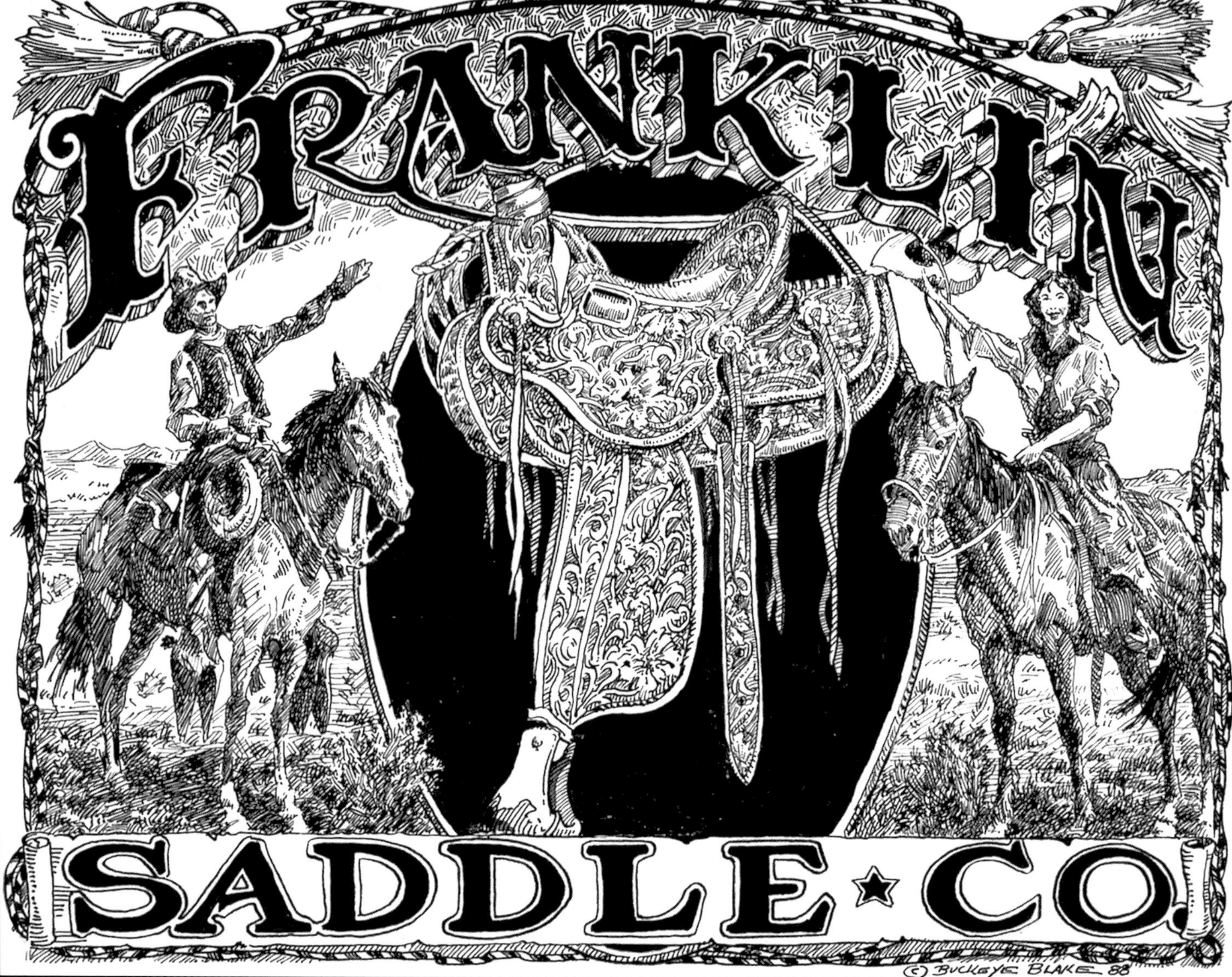
FRANKLIN
SADDLE ★ CO.
© BUCKEYE BLAKE 88

During Blake's years of working different jobs, he found work as a sign painter, an occupation that has been the entry job for many American artists. This early on-the-job training had an important influence on Blake's career. The merger of word and image is an important characteristic of his work. In signpainting, this merger is a necessity. The word carries the message; the image attracts the attention. Blake continues to produce works which can serve as signs, such as the *Franklin Saddle Company,* 1988 (Plate 20). This pen-and-ink work uses a balanced composition with riders flanking the saddle and gesturing to the name. The dominant image is the saddle, set off against the black, oval background. The style of the lettering evokes the style of the saddle with its graphic exuberance in the tooled designs. The sign and its subject echo each other.

The combination of word and image led, logically, to the work of poster design. One of Blake's earliest posters was a design for an Augusta, Montana, rodeo in 1980. For the Cowboy Poetry Gathering in Elko, Nevada, Blake was commissioned to design the poster for the 1988 event, *The Fourth Cowboy Poetry Gathering,* 1987 (Plate 21). Blake is an appropriate choice to design the poster for the Elko event. The Poetry Gathering brings together cowboys and lovers of western culture in a celebration of a western artform that is traditional but has seen a revival that includes contemporary interpretations. For the poster Blake used several types of lettering for the words and incorporated the shape of the state of Nevada into the design.

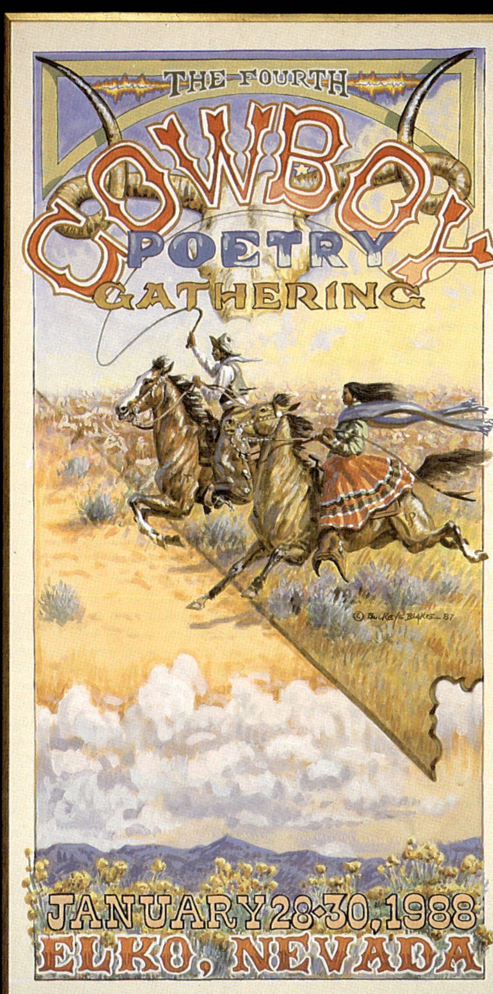

Plate 21:
The Fourth Cowboy Poetry Gathering, 1987.
Gouache on illustration board; 29 3/8 x 15 11/16 inches.
Loan from Sam and Denise Abell.

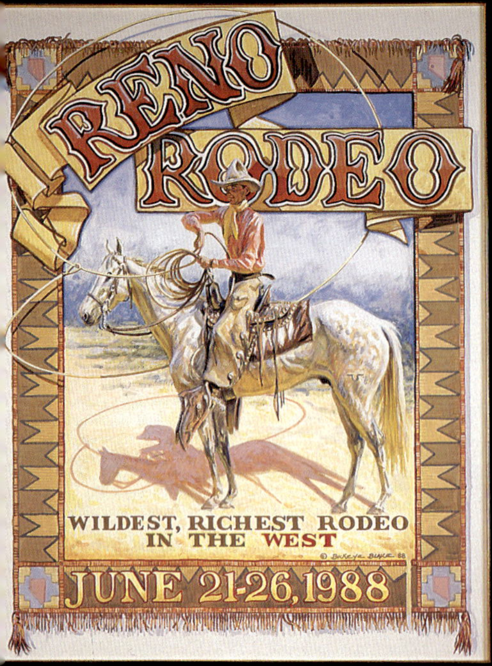

Top Left
Plate 22:
Reno Rodeo, 1988.
Gouache on illustration board;
28 x 22 inches.
Loan from Mr. and Mrs. Robert L. Noland.

Right
Plate 23:
Montana Game Wardens: A Century of Service, 1989.
Gouache on illustration board;
27 1/4 x 21 1/2 inches.
Loan from Broken O Ranch, William E. Moore - owner.

In planning a poster for the Reno Nevada, Rodeo, Blake submitted several designs, each with a different focus: a standing cowboy in woolly chaps; a traditional bucking horse and rider; a cowboy waving his hat; and Blake's favorite—which became the final version—a trick roper on horseback. In the final version of *Reno Rodeo,* 1988 (Plate 22) the lettering for the name of the rodeo appears on ribbons encircled by the rope's loop. For the *Montana Game Wardens: A Century of Service,* 1989 (Plate 23) Blake used the motif of an old-fashioned photographic mount as a framing device. The scene within the frame is portrayed more realistically than Blake's other poster designs. In a forest the horseback game warden pauses to check on a calf elk. Light breaks through the trees behind the warden, backlighting the scene while the elk rests peacefully in the shadows. In the poster the past frames contemporary reality.

Blake's recent poster design for the western musical group *Riders in the Sky,* 1992 (Plate 24) echoes the multiple layers of narrative and playfulness of the trio. The group revives western music of the 1930s and 1940s and gently parodies the singing cowboy phenomenon and western B-movies in their radio and television programs. In a format inspired by movie posters, Blake's image features portrait vignettes of Woody Paul, Ranger Doug, and Too Slim near the center of the composition with the name of the group arcing above the portraits. Below the three portraits Blake painted a scene from one of their stories. The three Riders having captured bank robbers, their sidekick bounces a biscuit off a bad guy's head. Above the name is a frieze of the three Riders on horseback and the sidekick on his wagon labeled with the Riders in the Sky catch phrase, "The Cowboy Way." The parodies of the musical group are paralleled in the poster design.

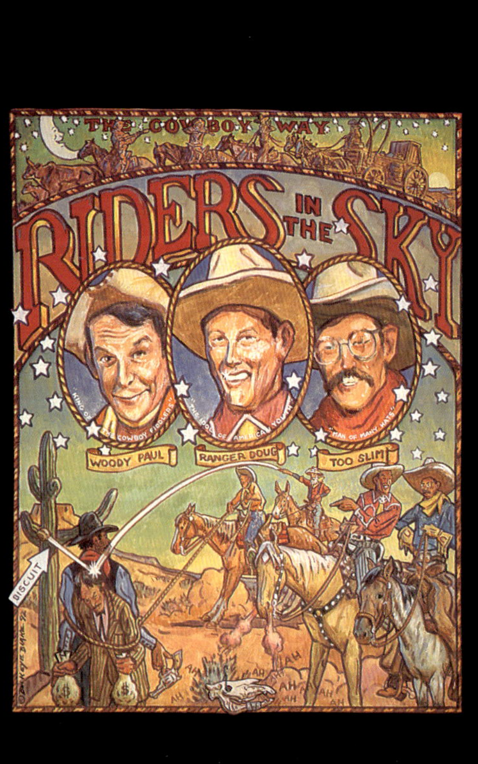

Bottom Left
Plate 24:
Riders in the Sky, 1992.
Gouache on illustration board;
30 x 24 inches.
From the Collection of Too Slim's Mercantile.

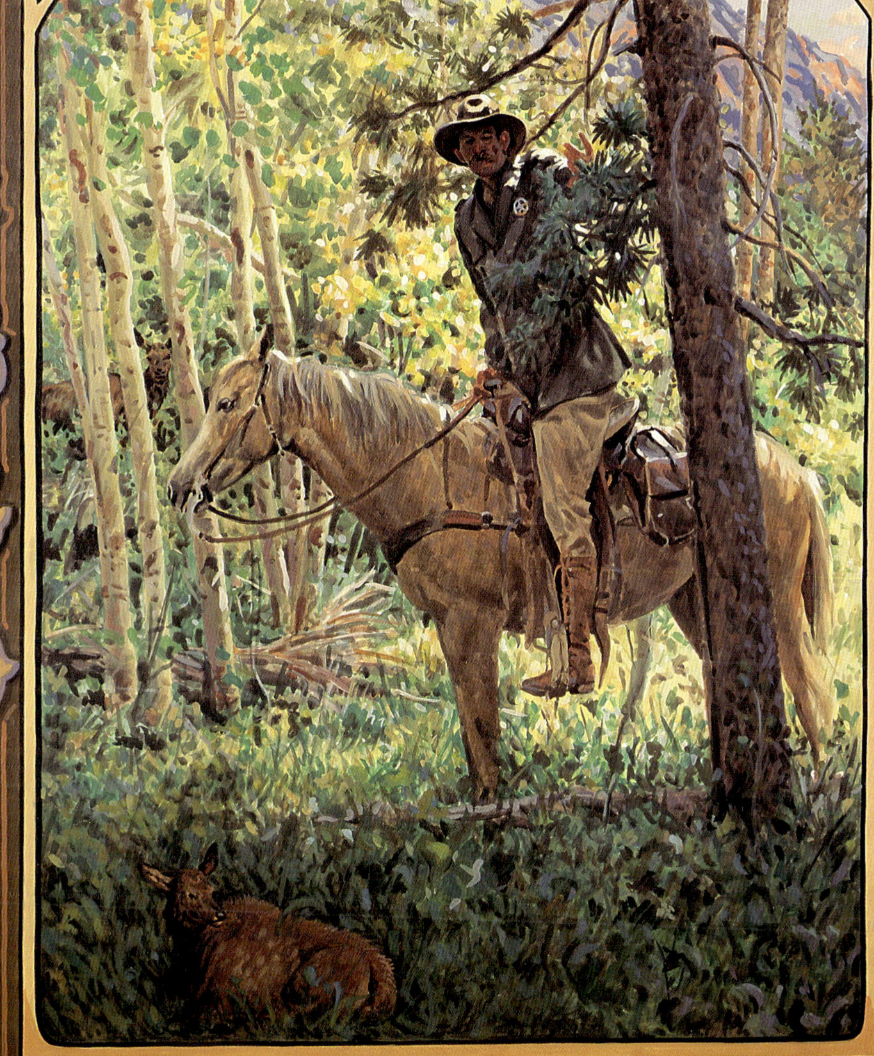
MONTANA
GAME WARDENS
1889
1989
A CENTURY OF
SERVICE
SPONSORED BY THE - BROKEN O RANCH - SIMMS, MONTANA

Plate 25:
Arizona, 1989.
Gouache on illustration board;
19 5/8 x 28 1/8 inches.
Loan from Mr. and Mrs. Richard Corcilius.

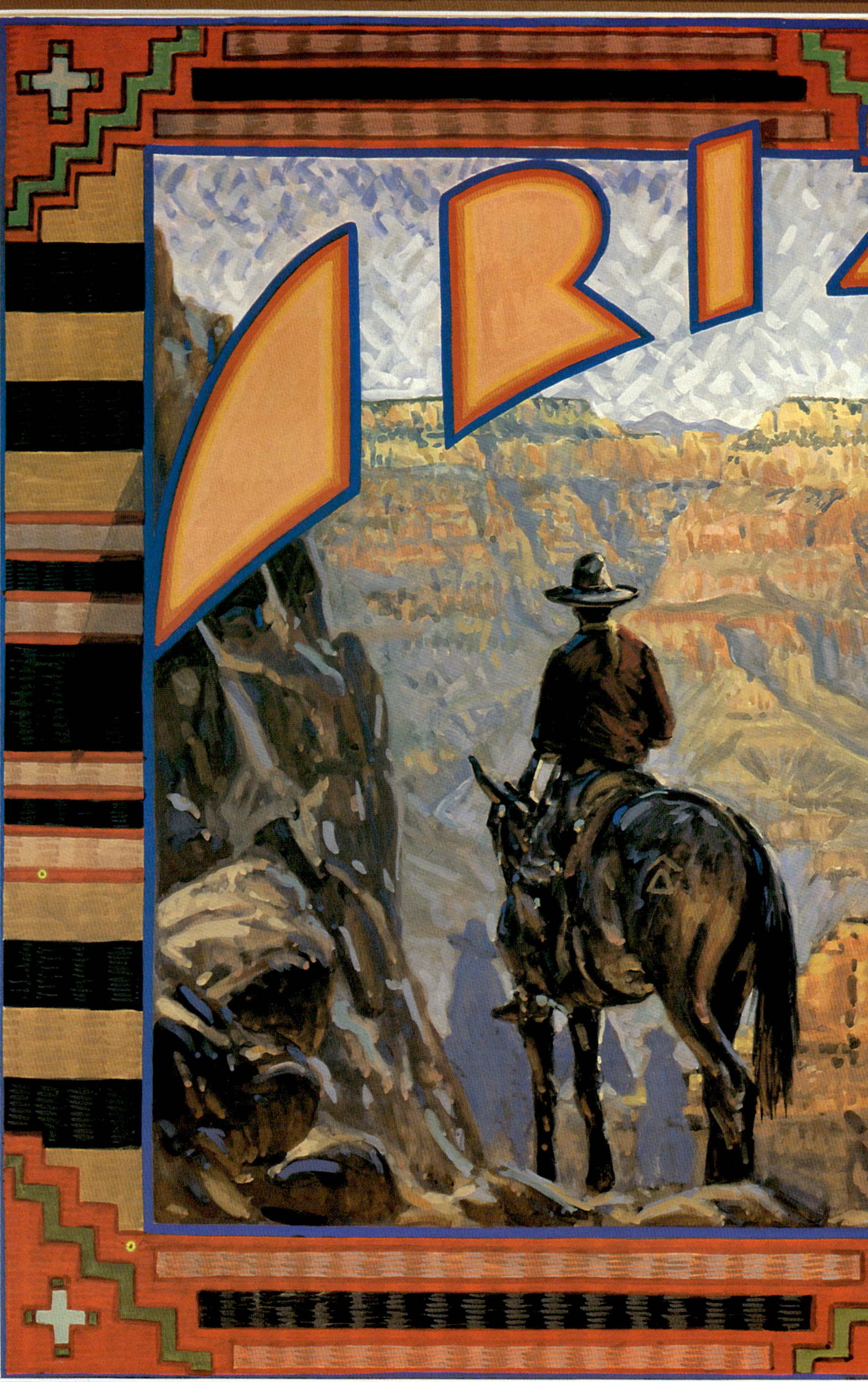

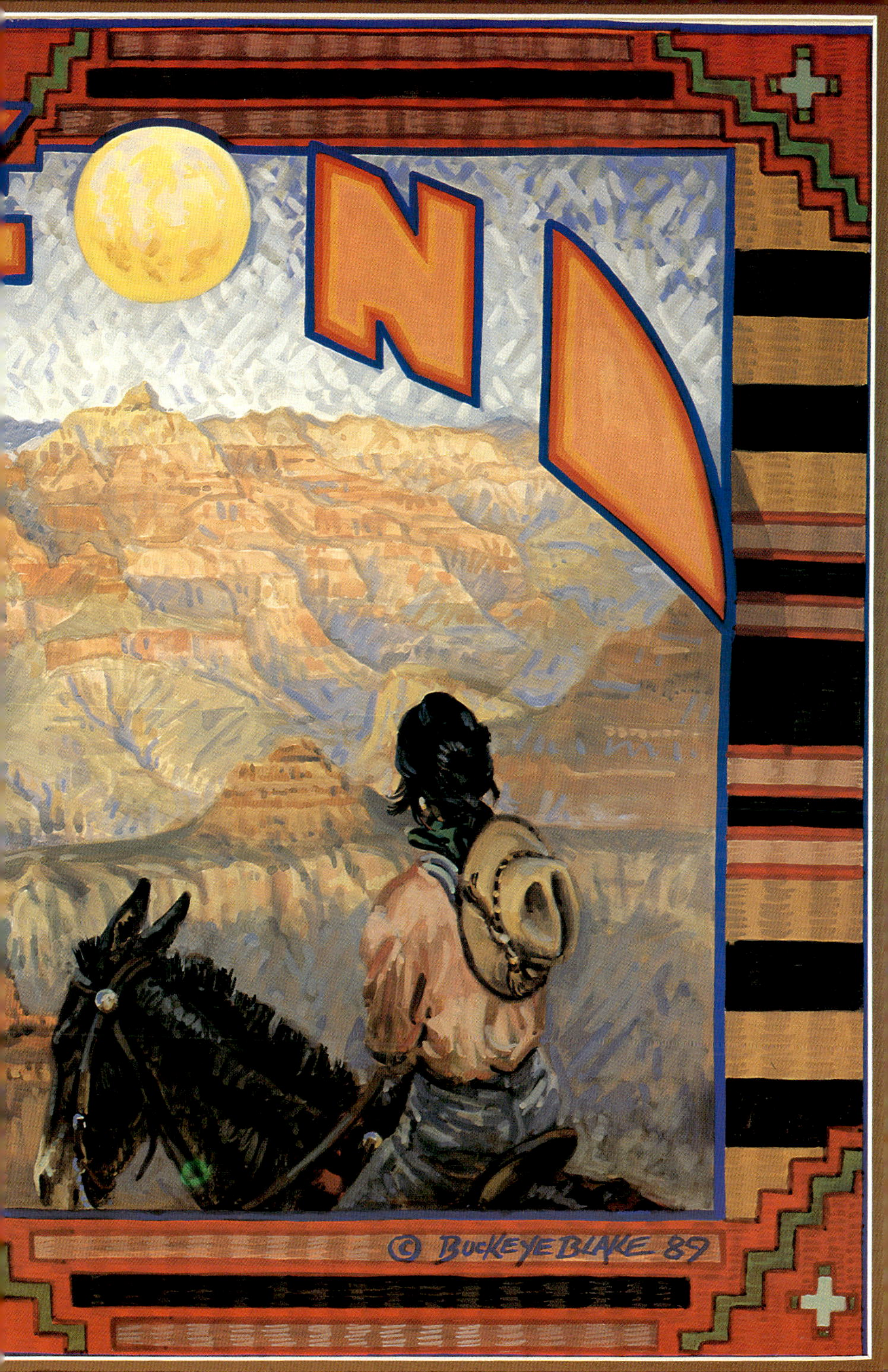
© BUCKEYE BLAKE 89

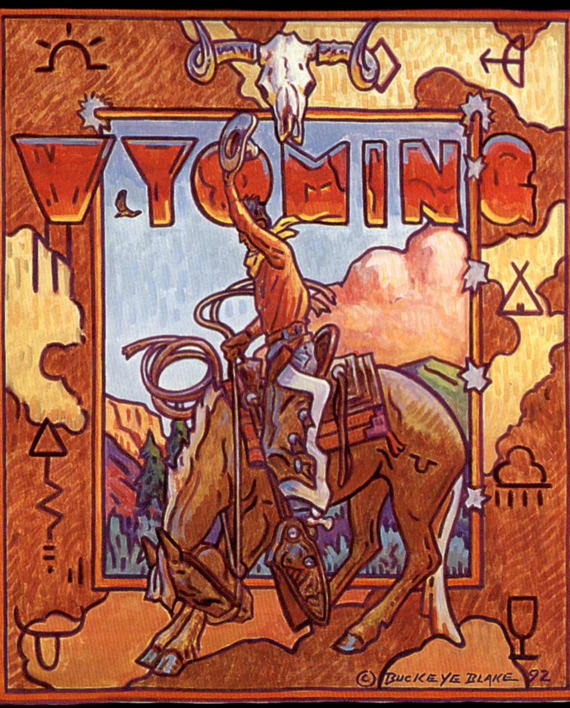

Plate 26:
Wyoming, 1992.
Gouache on illustration board; 26 x 22 ½ inches.
Loan from Anonymous Collector, Wapiti, Wyoming.

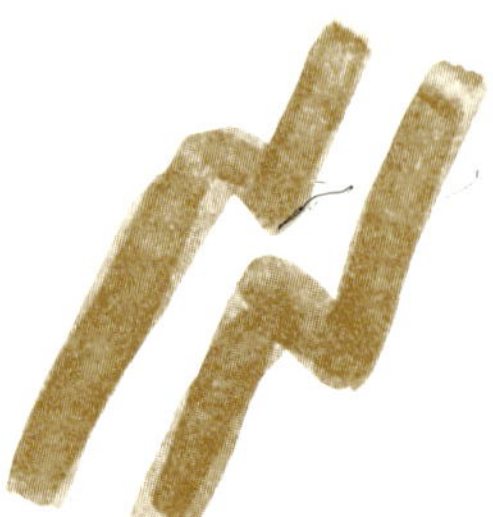

Buckeye's interest in combining image and text in a poster led him to create other works of art which draw upon the poster format, but which were not commissioned to announce specific events. In 1989 he designed *Arizona* (Plate 25, preceding page), a gouache painting which evokes the tourist advertisements of the 1930s. An Indian blanket design frames a scene of the Grand Canyon with a cowboy and cowgirl riding mules down into the canyon. Arced over the scene appear the letters spelling out "Arizona." Three years later he produced another painting from the state poster concept, this time for the northern state *Wyoming*, 1992 (Plate 26). A faux-cowhide border frames a landscape over which the lettering for Wyoming is superimposed. Over that is superimposed a cowboy on a bucking horse, a variation on the state symbol of bucking horse and rider. In contrast with the deep space of Arizona, Blake used a surface layering for the Wyoming image. The *Wyoming* painting also features a strongly pronounced outline and little true modeling. Form is indicated by the shape and by occasional lines to indicate folds. Blake employs this strongly linear style in other works, such as *On The Western Front*, 1991 (Plate 27). The stylization created by the bold purple lines serves as a reminder that the cowboy is an image.

Right
Plate 27:
On the Western Front, 1991.
Gouache on illustration board;
19 15/16 x 13 9/16 inches.
Loan from Jim and Sue King, Chicago, Illinois.

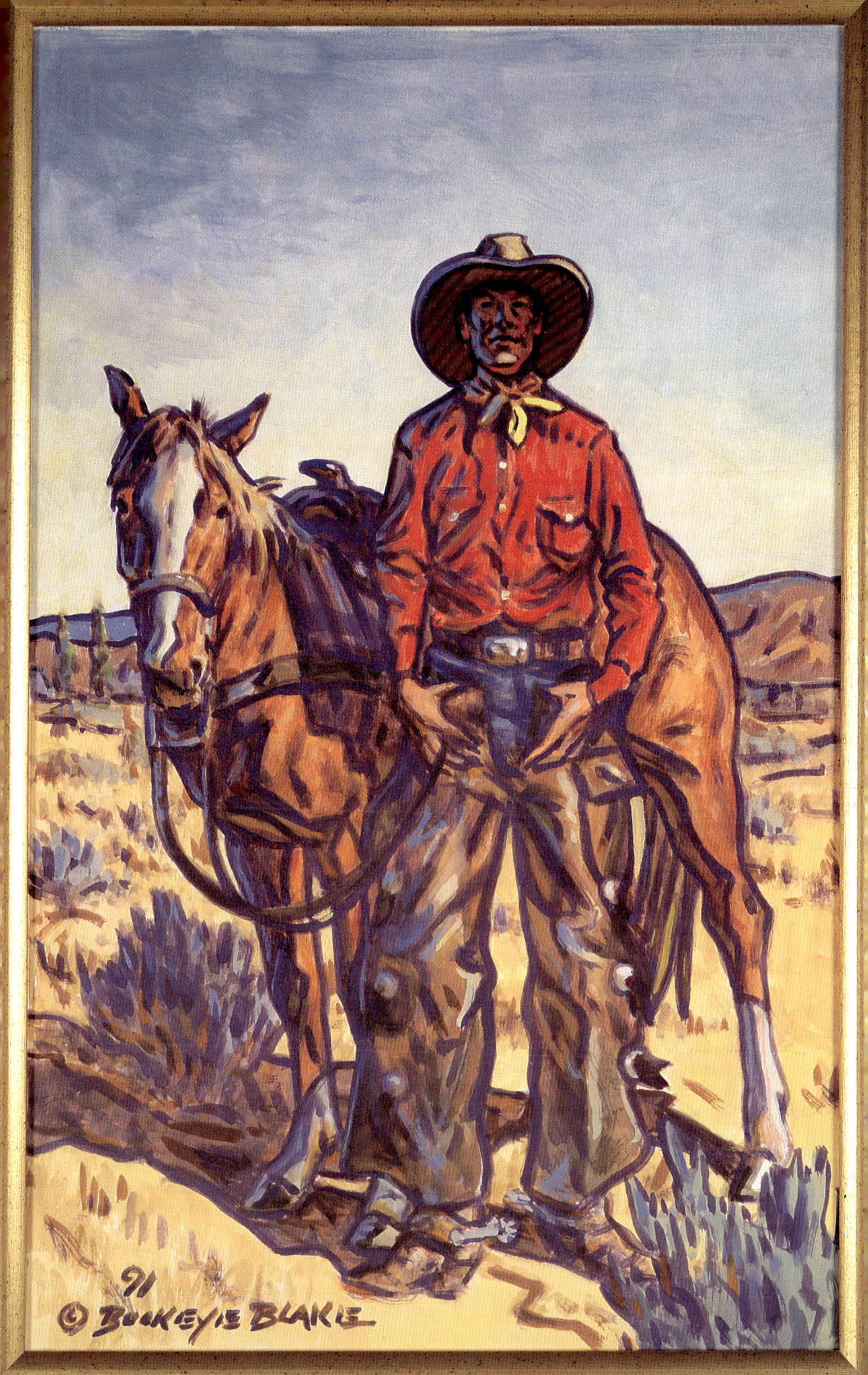
91
© BUCKEYE BLAKE

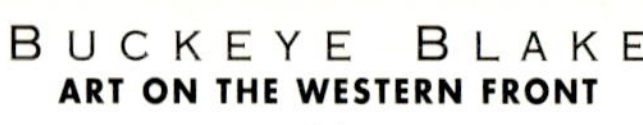

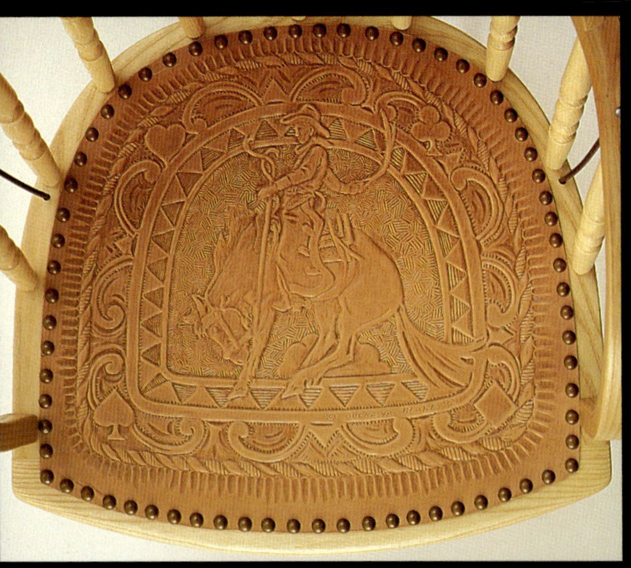

Chair (detail of seat), 1993.
Wood and embossed leather; 29 x 20 x 23 inches.
Loan from Due-West Furniture, Rindge, New Hampshire.

Stool (detail of seat), 1993.
Wood and embossed leather;
24 1/2 x 17 x 17 inches.
Loan from Due-West Furniture, Rindge, New Hampshire.

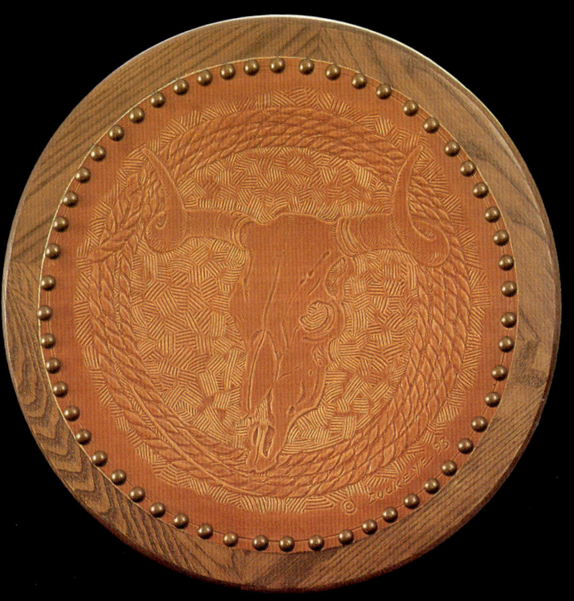

Blake's interest in iconic images of the states such as Arizona and Wyoming may derive from an early commission. In 1980 he designed a series of 50 whiskey decanters, each one symbolizing one of the states. The artist has maintained an interest in designing decorative arts objects, in part due to his pragmatic approach to making art. He likes an art that is functional. Blake has produced designs for pottery, clothing, and furniture, both for unique works which he makes himself and also for mass-produced works intended for a larger audience (Composite Plate 28). He quite literally finds a canvas in the material for handbags and makes a portable art in his hand-painted handbags.

Right
Plate 28:
Chair, 1993.
Wood and embossed leather;
29 x 20 x 23 inches.

Stool, 1993.
Wood and embossed leather;
24 1/2 x 17 x 17 inches.
Loans from Due-West Furniture,
Rindge, New Hampshire.

Stars 'n' Cowgirls and *Saddle and Rope Scarves*, 1990.
Silk; 33 x 33 inches.
Buffalo Bill Historical Center,
Cody, Wyoming.
Gifts of Cattle Kate.

Painted Bag, 1993.
Acrylic and marker on canvas;
13 1/2 x 19 x 9 inches.
Loan courtesy Big Horn Gallery,
Cody, Wyoming.

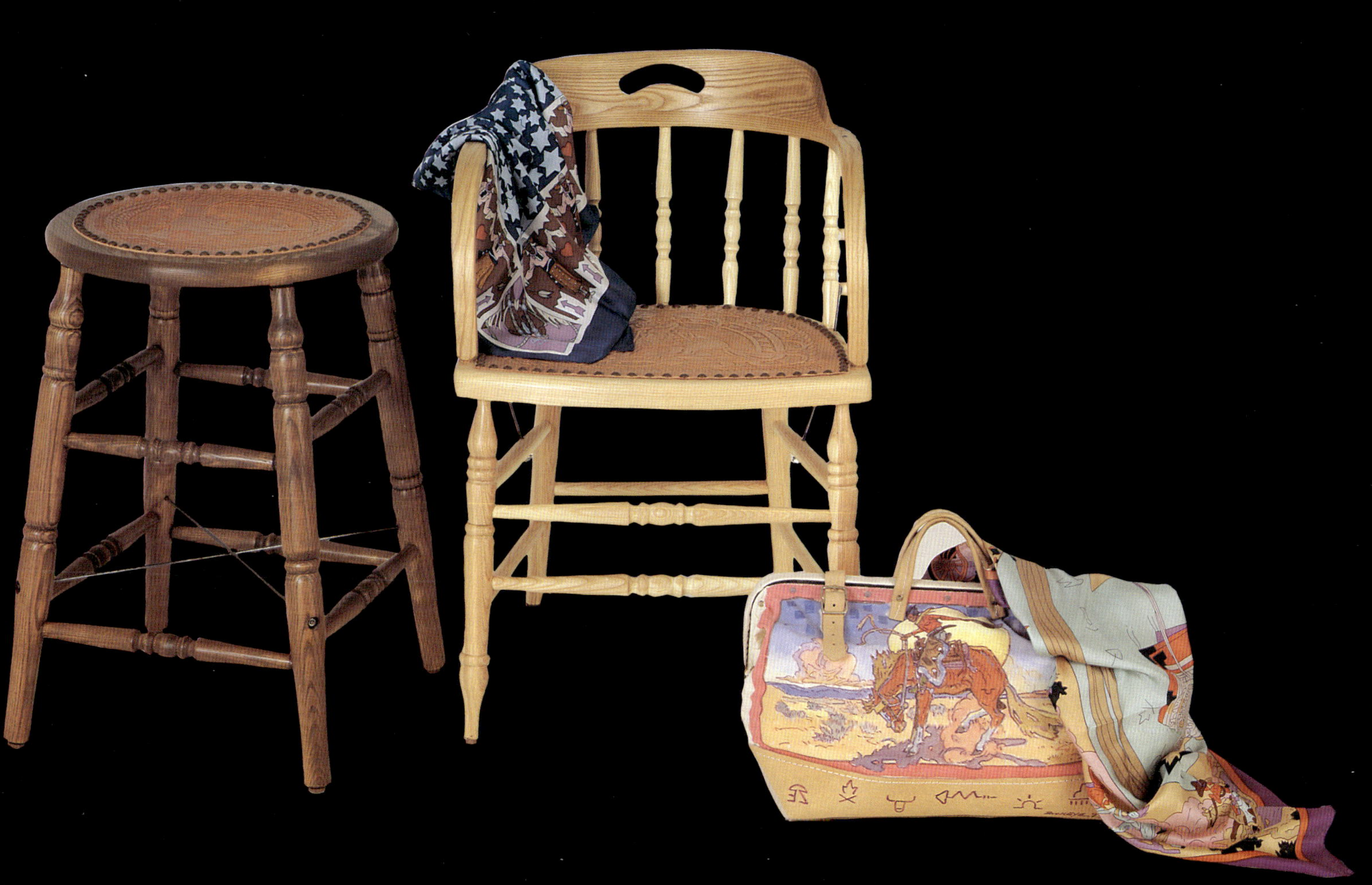

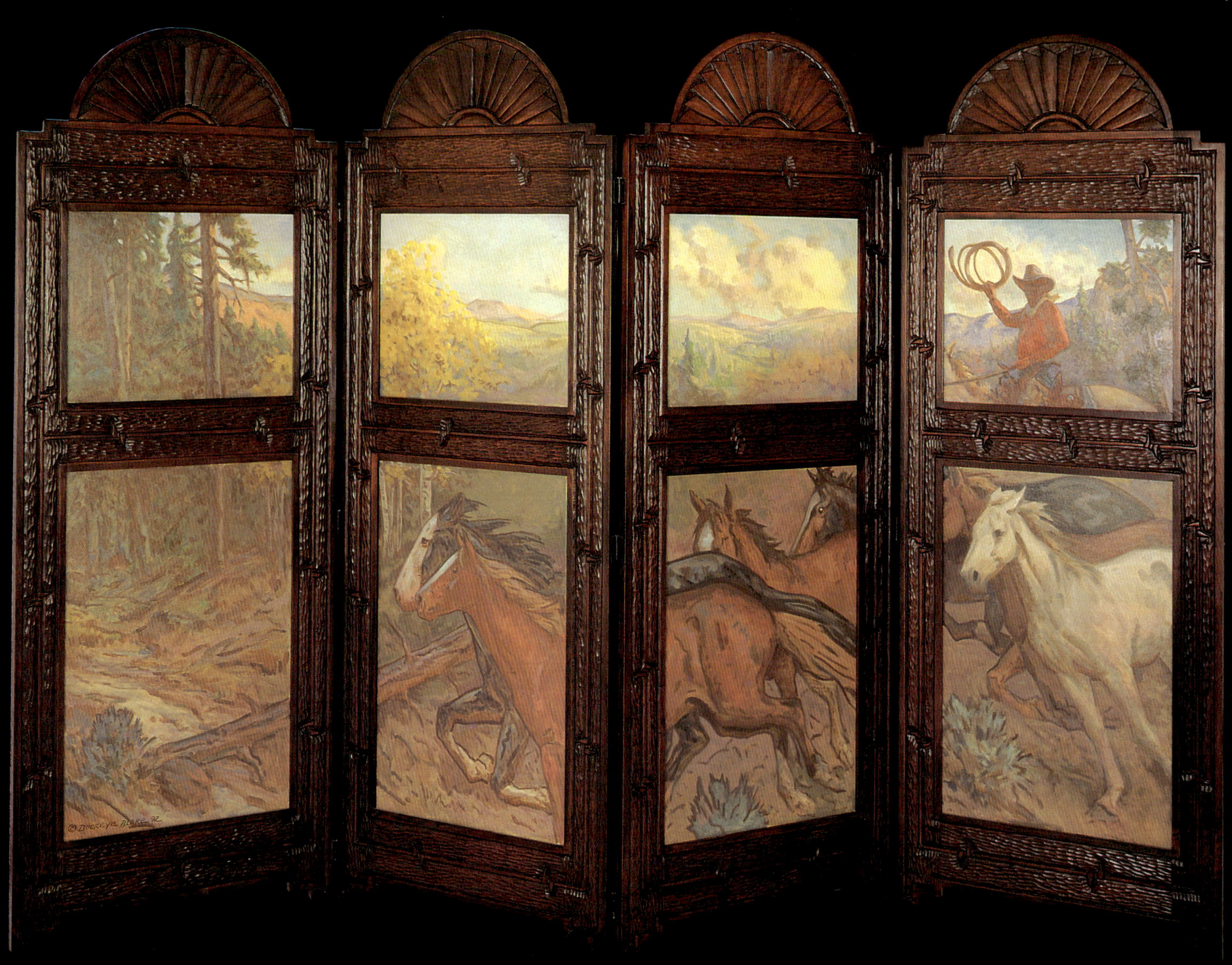

Plate 29:
Wild Horses, 1992.
Oil on canvas board in wooden frame carved by Milo Marks; 74 x 110 1/2 inches.
Loan from Anne L. Pattee.

One of his most successful new forays into functional artistic objects is the folding screen, *Wild Horses,* 1992 (Plate 29). Many 19th and 20th century artists have been challenged by the folding screen format. The folding screen contains the flat surface of a painting, yet it is a practical piece of furniture. Blake collaborated with furniture maker Milo Marks of Meridian, Texas, who carved the screen following Blake's ideas. Blake had met Marks at an exposition in conjunction with a cutting horse show and saw in the carver's work the style he wanted. Blake sent instructions to Marks saying he wanted an effect that was rustic, yet elegant. Marks used a vocabulary of western design elements such as barbed wire and sunbursts. The structure of a screen presents the artist with the choice of making separate painted scenes for each panel or of painting one continuous image. Blake chose the single composition, using the screen's frame as a window. The painted portion of the screen consists of four parts, a continuous scene of wild horses being herded out of the mountains. In a preliminary drawing, Blake first used a more static composition with little apparent movement; a cowboy lopes with a herd of horses (Plate 30). In the final version, the horses gallop away from the rope-swinging cowboy. The flowing composition, with its theme of captured wildness, is contained by the structure of the wooden frame. The work with Marks is one of several projects in which Blake has collaborated with another artist, using the skills of each to bring forth the best work from both.

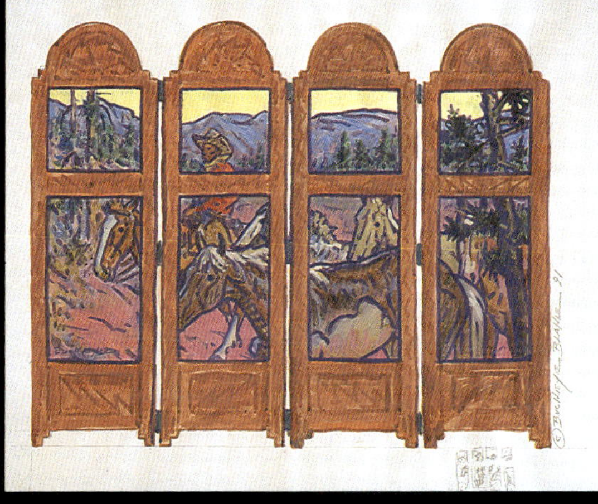

Plate 30:
Preliminary drawing for *Wild Horses* screen, 1991.
Gouache on paper; 11 x 13 15/16 inches.
Loan from the Collection of Buckeye Blake.

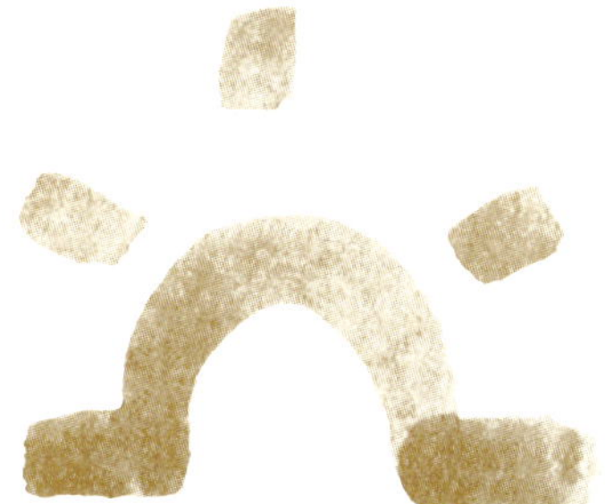

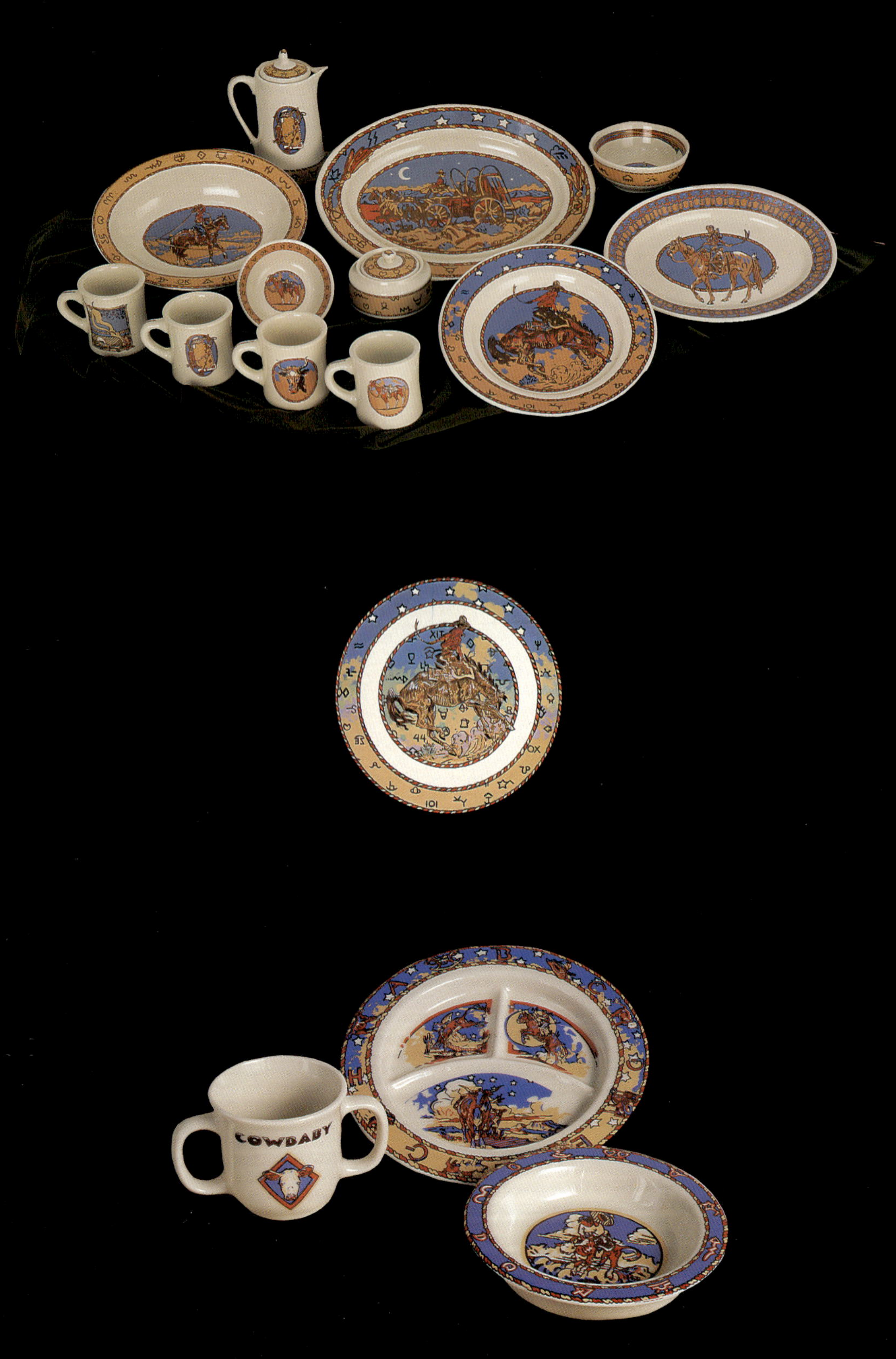

Top Left
Plate 31:
Cow Camp China, 1990.
A selection of pieces including
12 1/2 and 15 5/8 inch platters.
Loan from the Collection of Buckeye Blake.

Center Left:
Plate 32:
Design for *Cow Camp China*, 1990.
Gouache on illustration board;
24 x 24 inches.
Loan from the Collection of Buckeye Blake.

Blake has also designed objects for mass-production. In these designs he extends art into the realm of the everyday, and produces western design objects which can be used to create a totally western environment. Blake's *Cow Camp China*, 1990 (Plate 31) echoes the dude-ranch-style pottery of artists such as Till Goodan. With his *Cowbaby China*, 1992 (Plate 33) for children Blake has created a character the "cowbaby," whose adventures in the West are told in narratives accompanying the pottery.

Bottom Left:
Plate 33:
Cowbaby China, 1992.
Divided plate: 8 3/8 inches in diameter;
bowl: 6 1/2 inches in diameter;
cup: 3 3/8 inches in diameter.
Loan from "Dudettes" Tona Blake and Laurie McGuane.

Right
Plate 34:
Cow Camp China, 1990.
11 inch diameter dinner plate.
Loan from the Collection of Buckeye Blake.

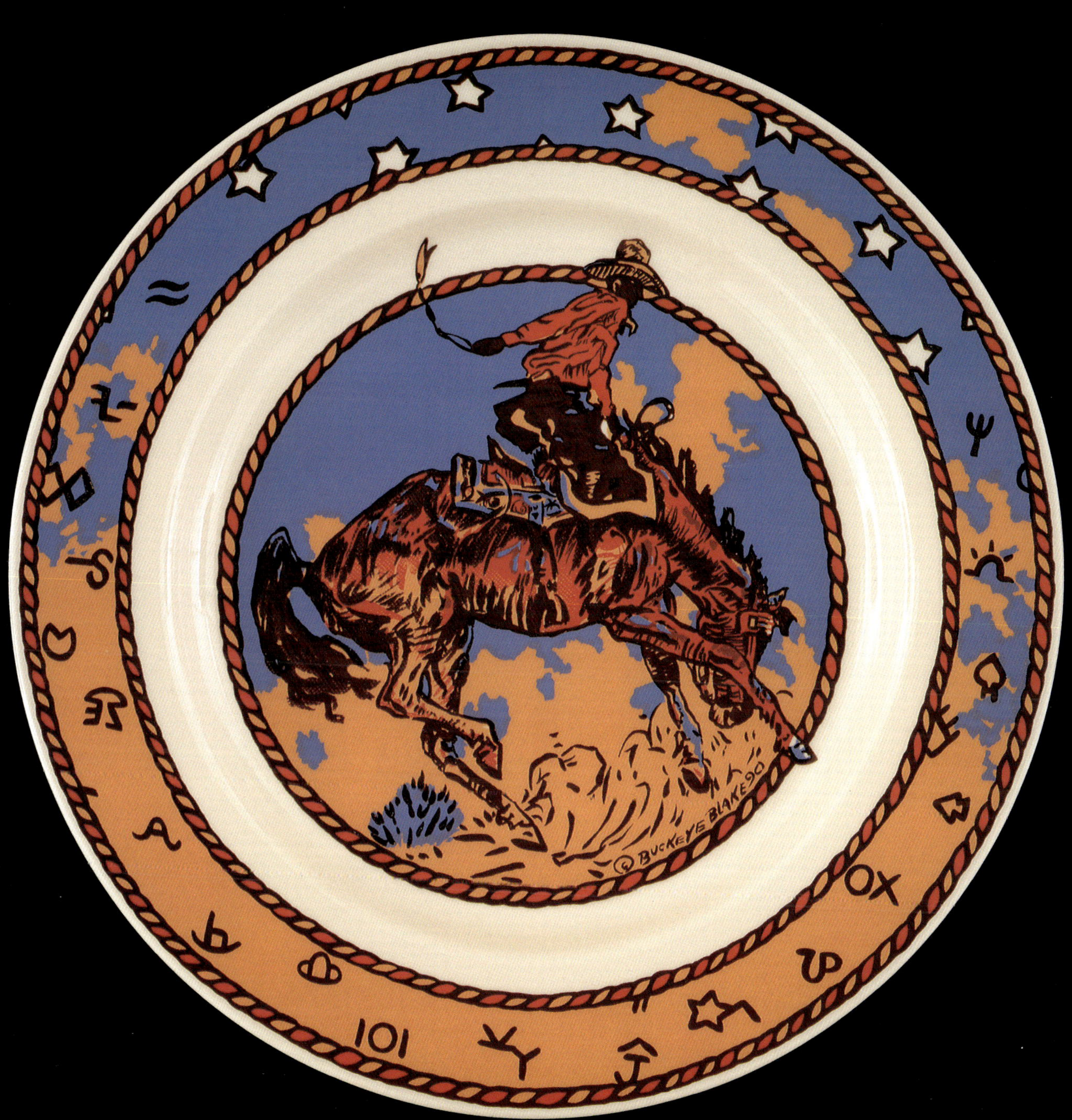
© BUCKEYE BLAKE 90
OX
101

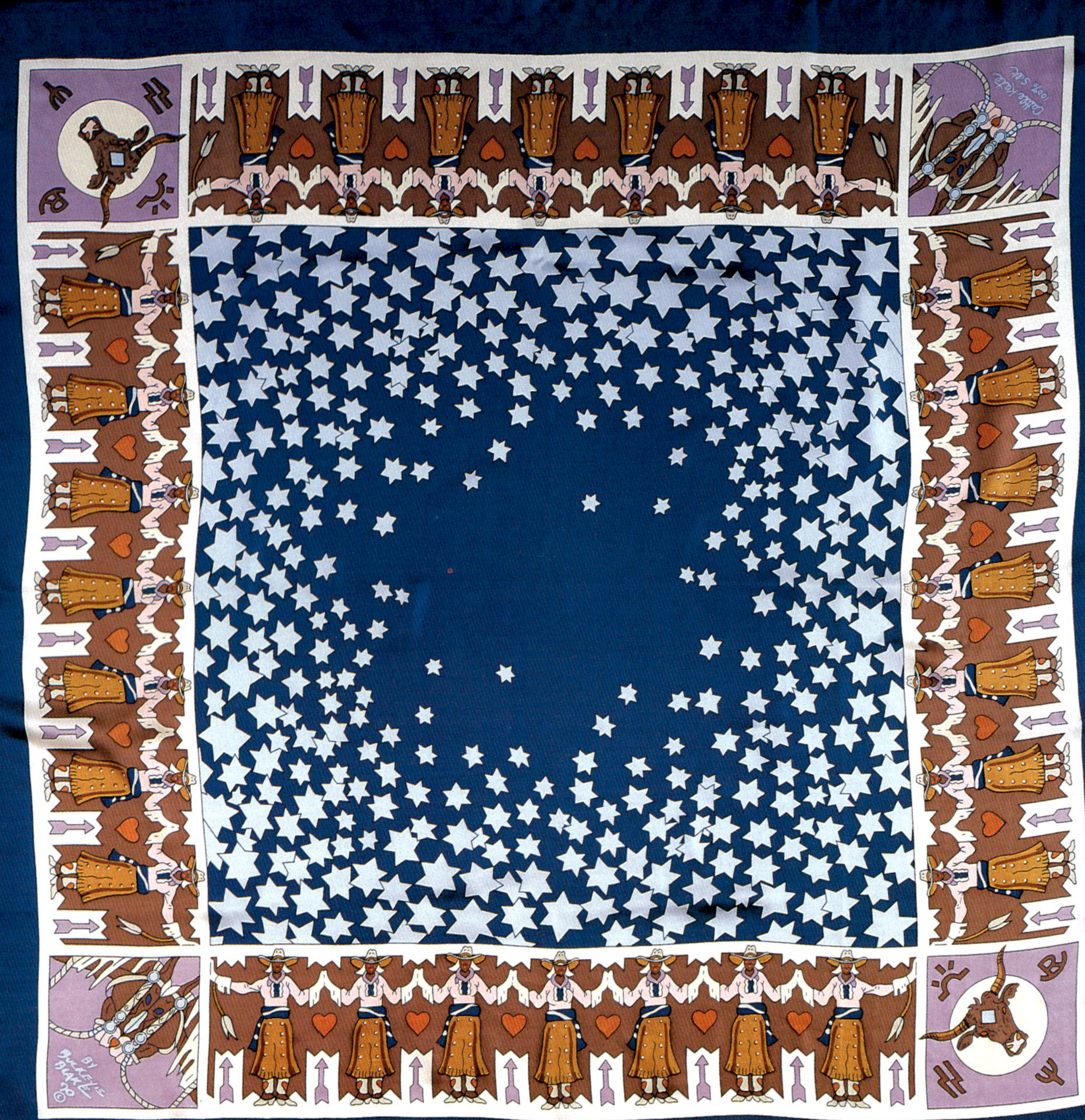

Left
Plate 35:
Stars 'n' Cowgirls Scarf, 1990.
Silk; 33 x 33 inches.
Buffalo Bill Historical Center, Cody, Wyoming.
Gift of Cattle Kate.

Blake's commercial work points to the importance of western design of the 1930s and 1940s, especially the influence of Jo Mora, the California artist and designer whose graphic images populate the western vocabulary. Blake's design for scarves for the Cattle Kate clothing company uses repetitive cowgirls reminiscent of Mora's figures (Plate 37). Drawing upon the past as well is Blake's latest design for manufactured furniture. Working with a company called Southwest Design, Blake has designed Due-West furniture, which reproduces a western saloon chair and related stool. As a prototype, Blake used a chair that he had in his studio along with saddles and other western gear. The chair appears in paintings such as *Winter out the Window*, 1986 (Plate 36), Blake's version of the classic western cardgame. For the seats of the chair and stool, Blake designed western motifs to be embossed onto leather, a bronc rider for the chair (Preface) and a cattle skull for the stool (back cover).

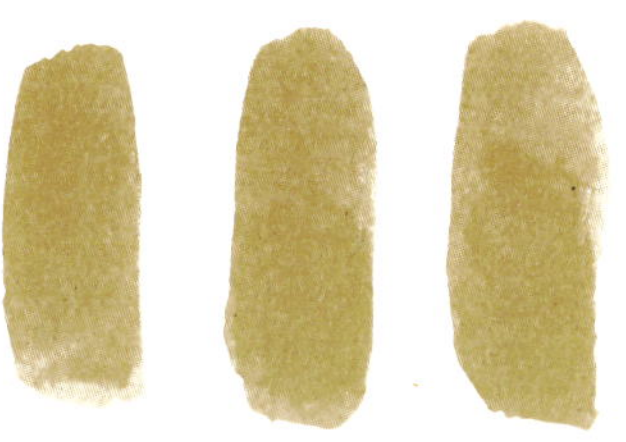

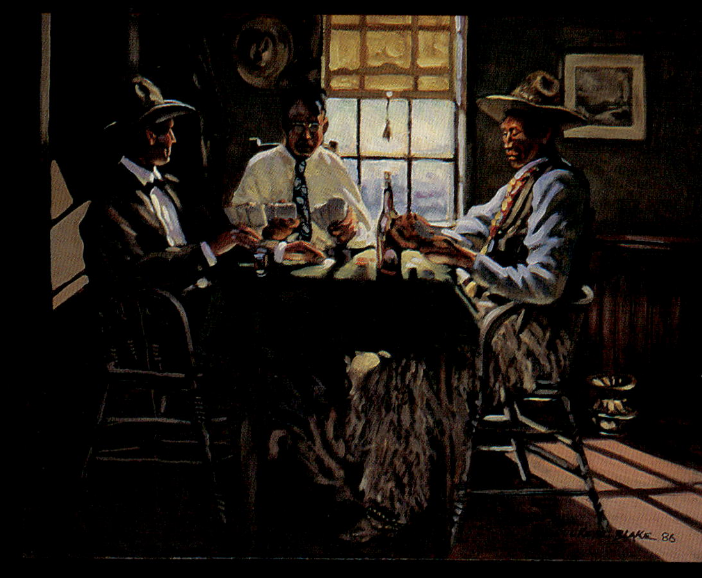

Plate 36:
Winter out the Window, 1986.
Oil on board;
20 1/16 x 26 inches.
Loan from the Collection of Stephen Scott.

Plate 37:
Drawing for *Stars 'n' Cowgirls Scarf,* 1989.
Pencil, marker, and gouache on illustration board;
15 5/16 x 20 inches.
Loan from the Collection of Buckeye Blake.

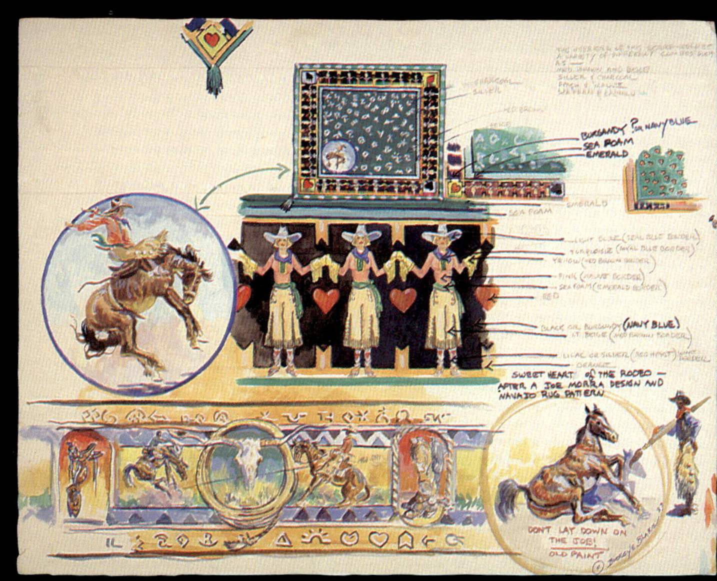

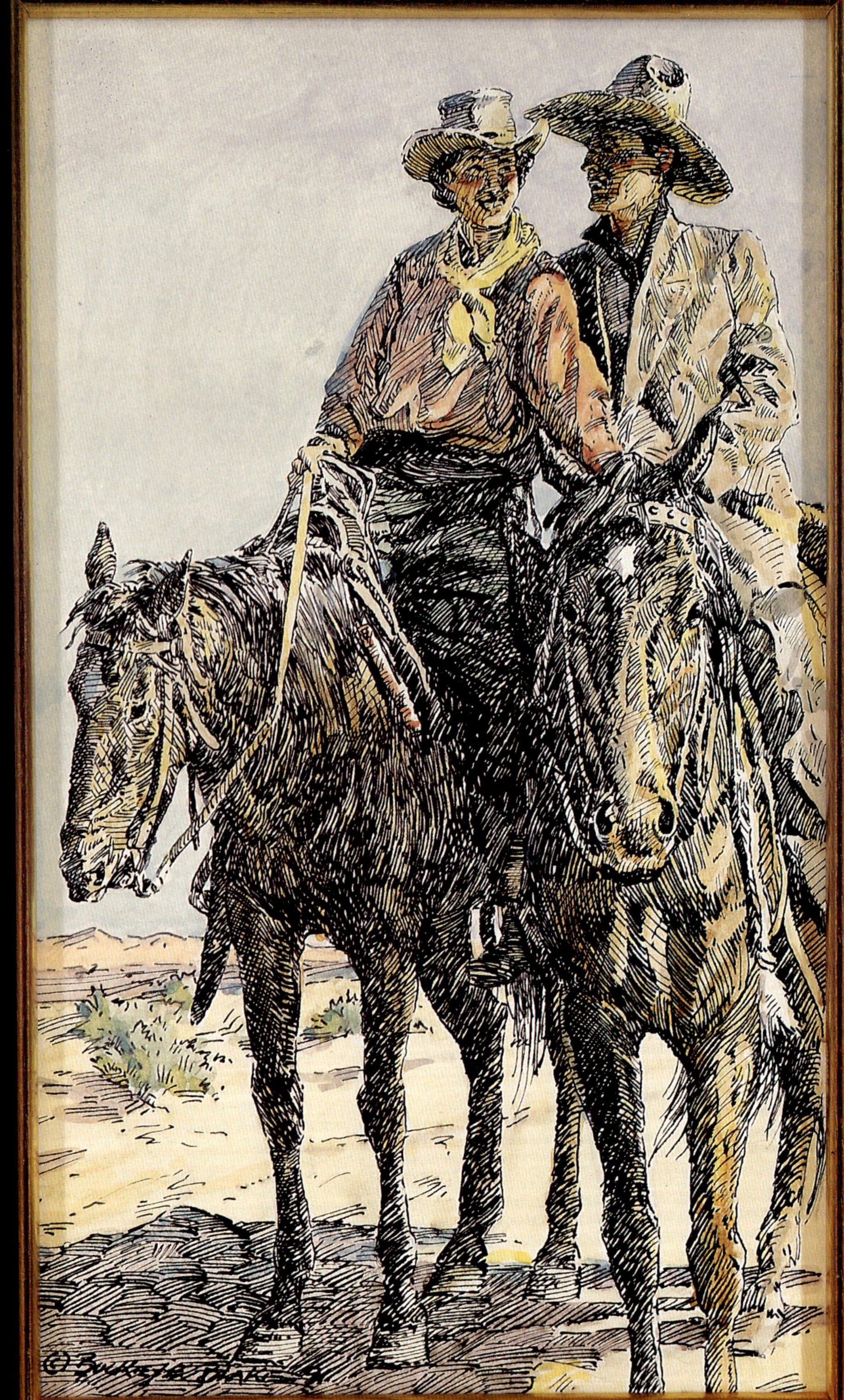

Plate 38:
Pitching Woo, 1991.
Watercolor, pen and ink
on illustration board;
9 3/4 x 5 7/8 inches.
Loan from the Collection of
Ms. Astrid Lundstrom.

While Blake's works sometimes convey a nostalgia for a West that we know is filtered through a romantic screen, his view of the contemporary West is a more inclusive world than that celebrated in western art of the past. While the cowboy is a dominant motif, the artist also makes room for the cowgirl. Watercolors such as *Pitching Woo,* 1991 (Plate 38) portray the element of romantic love that popular fiction and the movies made such an important element of the Western narrative. Blake revives the playful image of the cowgirl of the early 20th century in the scarf designs and in the delightful painted sculpture *Sweethearts of the Rodeo,* 1987 (Plate 39). Yet he also looks more closely at the roles of women in the West. The *Sweethearts* sculpture was inspired by looking at photographs of western women from the early 20th century, part of the research his wife Tona Freeman Blake was doing for a screenplay on the life of rodeo bronc rider Fannie Sperry Steele, a world champion in women's bucking horse competition. Steele's accomplishments in the rough rodeo world were important, but largely forgotten. Tona's research on Steele inspired Buckeye to paint several works with Fannie as the subject and he was commissioned to sculpt her portrait for the National Cowboy Hall of Fame (Plate 40).

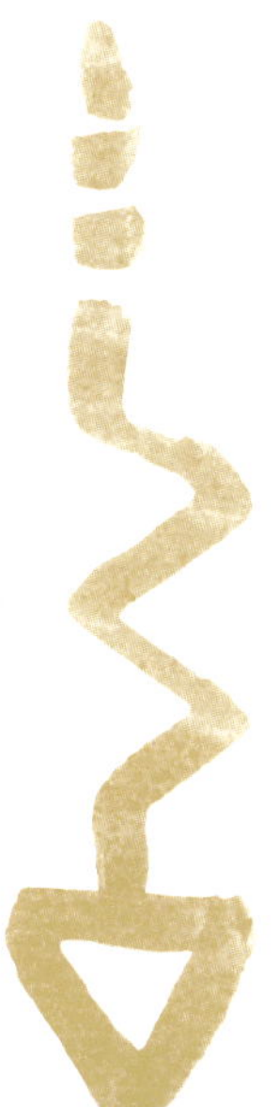

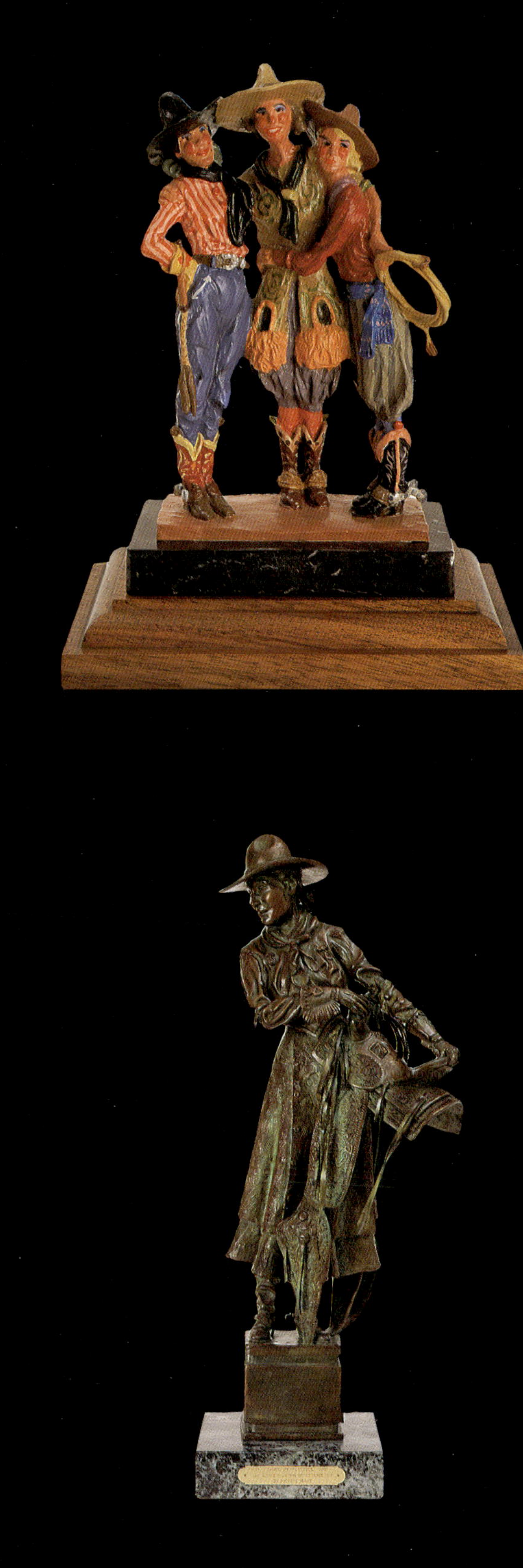

Plate 39:
Sweethearts of the Rodeo, 1987.
Bronze, painted; 9 x 6 x 3 inches.
Number 24 of an edition of 38.
Loan from Mr. and Mrs. Charles E. Cord.

Plate *40*:
Fannie Sperry Steele, 1982.
Bronze; 25 3/4 x 10 1/2 x 7 1/2 inches.
Artist's Proof of an edition of 12.
Loan from The Harmsen Collection.

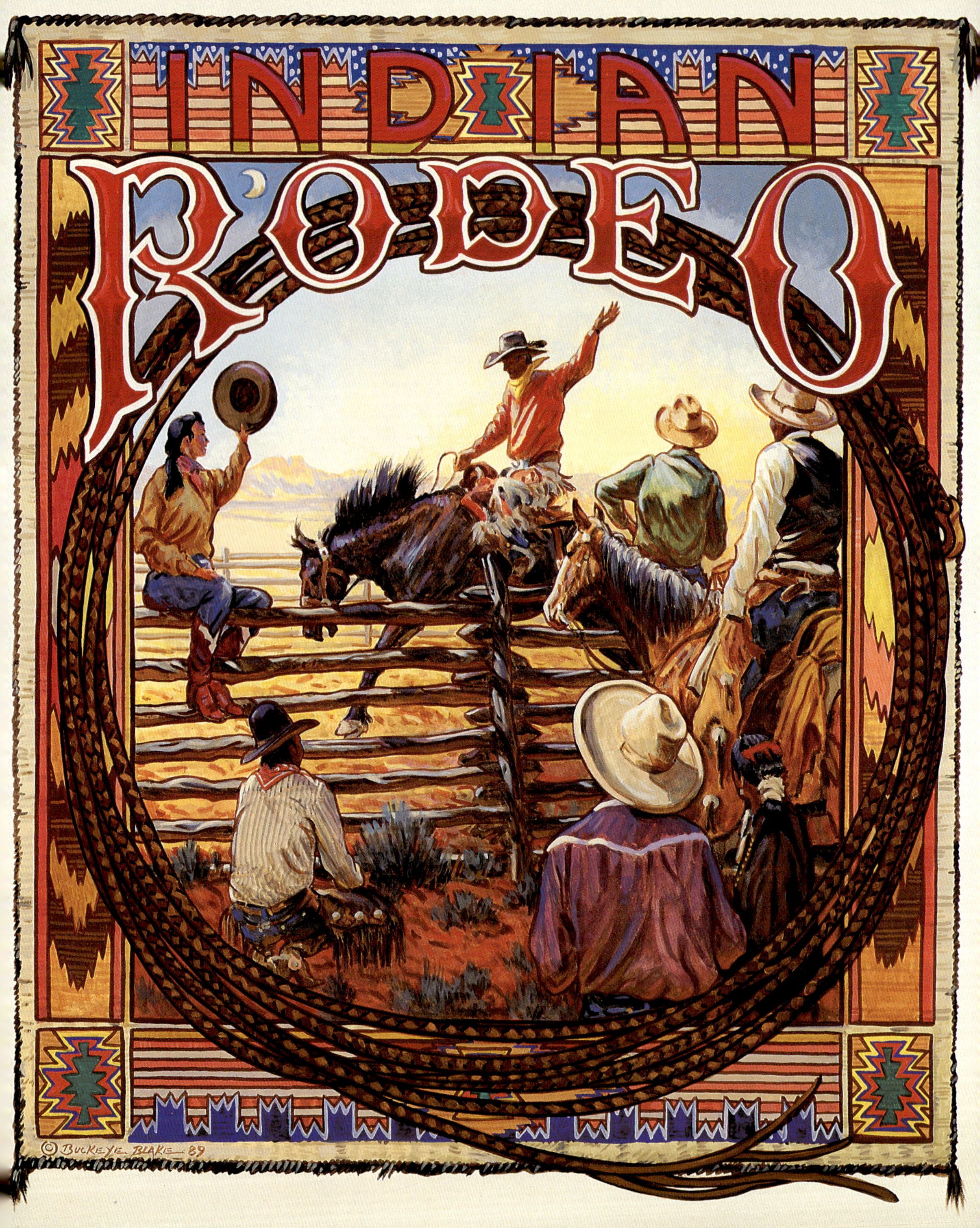
INDIAN
RODEO
© BUCKEYE BLAKE 89

Depictions of Indians in Blake's work go beyond the conventional in portraying aspects of contemporary life. *Indian Rodeo,* 1989 (Plate 41), one of Blake's paintings in the poster style, portrays the 20th century merging of cowboy-Indian life. The reservation period at the turn of the century put an effective end to the life of the Indian as hunter on the Plains. Since the days of Wild West exhibitions, Indians have participated in arena performances of riding skill. The horse culture of the traditional Plains tribes found expression in rodeo skills; this is celebrated in Blake's portrayal of Indian rodeo. The scene is doubly framed in a stepped design and a rope.

Blake also makes a place for Hispanics in his works. His Poetry Gathering poster used Hispanic figures to evoke the Spanish roots of cowboy culture. The artist has more recently developed a theme portraying the migrant workers who labor in the agricultural states of the West. Blake had wanted to do a series of paintings with a California setting which would evoke the feeling of the John Steinbeck era of the Dust Bowl and the migration from the Plains states to California. At a cutting horse show he met a patron from California who commissioned him to do paintings of the migrant workers in the state. In Salinas Valley, Blake did sketches of workers in the artichoke fields, which resulted in *The Tenders,* 1991, and *Dona Laguna,* 1991 (Plates 44, 42). The woman who modeled for *Dona Laguna* appears in other paintings such as *On the High Prairie,* 1991 (Plate 43) where Blake has placed her in a southwestern desert as a goatherd. These paintings silhouette the workers against the background of the landscape and their labor. Like the French 19th-century realist, Gustave Courbet, Blake treats his subjects with deliberate dignity.

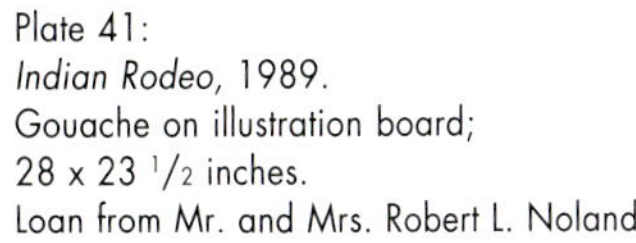

Plate 41:
Indian Rodeo, 1989.
Gouache on illustration board;
28 x 23 1/2 inches.
Loan from Mr. and Mrs. Robert L. Noland.

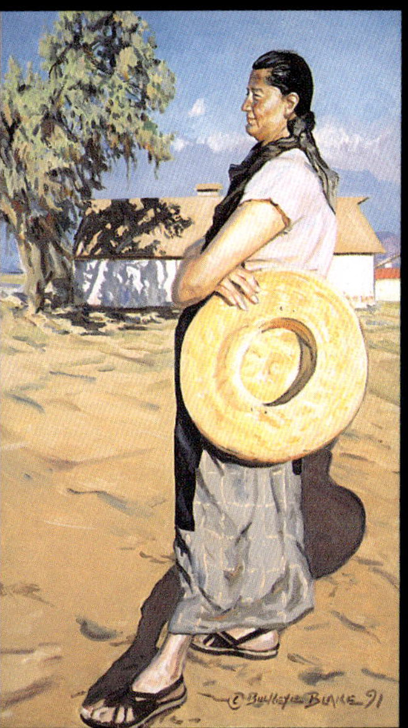

Plate 42:
Dona Laguna, 1991.
Oil on canvas; 47 5/8 x 27 1/2 inches.
Loan from the Collection of Dan W. Lufkin.

Plate 43:
On the High Prairie, 1991.
Gouache on illustration board; 21 x 29 1/2 inches.
Loan from Tom and Laurie McGuane.

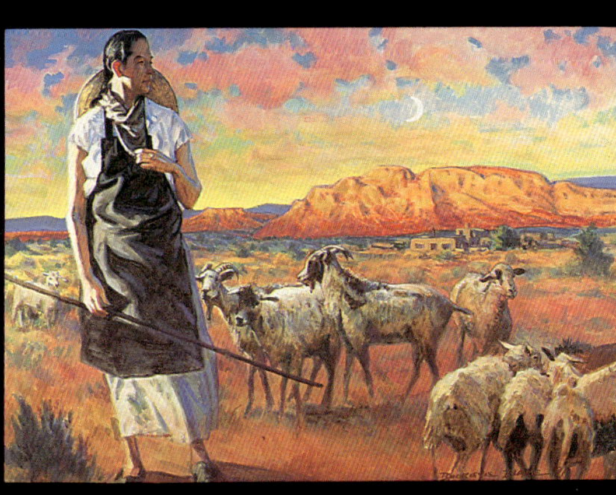

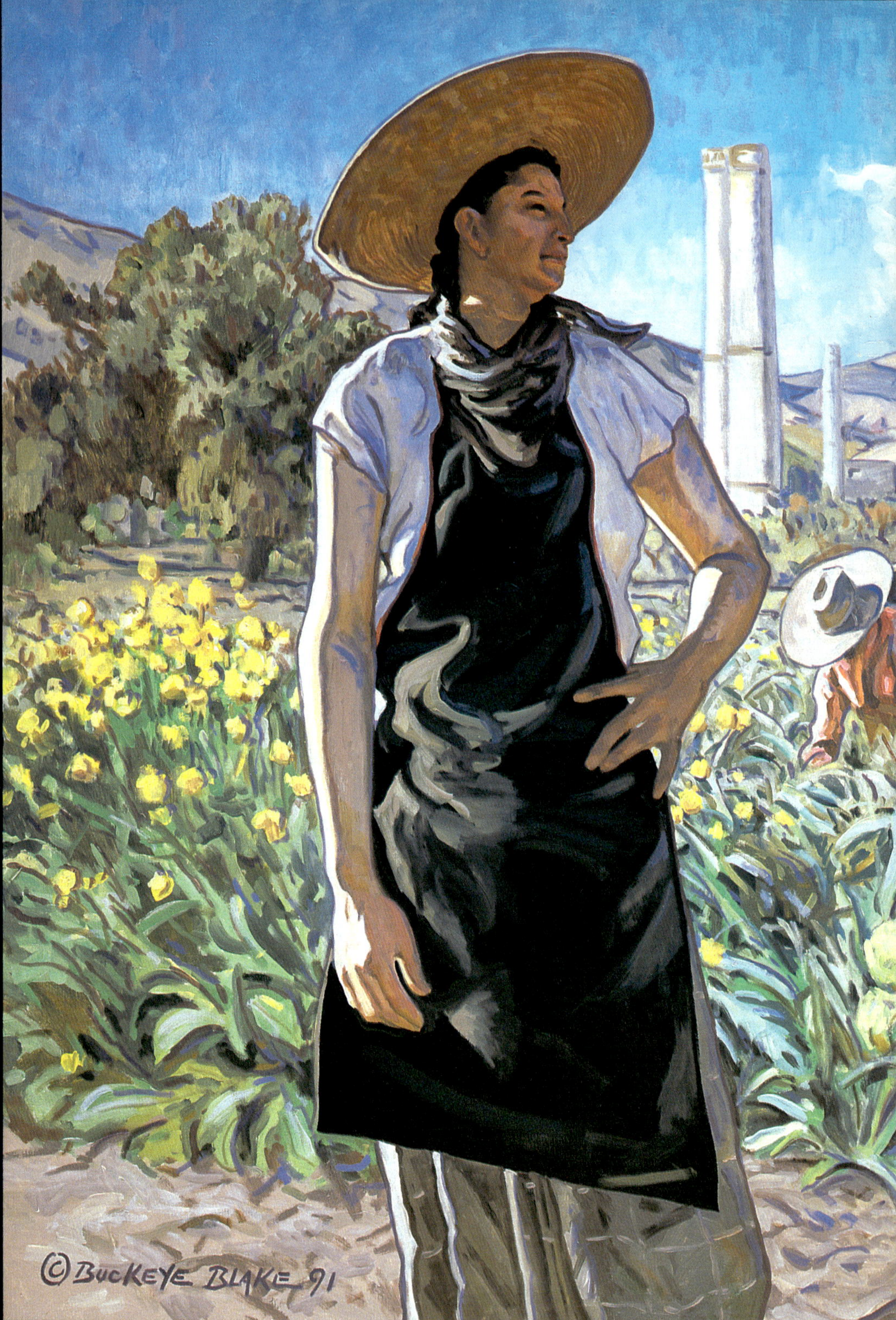

Plate 44:
The Tenders, 1991.
Oil on canvas; 47 x 71 $^1/_2$ inches.
Loan from the Collection of Dan W. Lufkin.

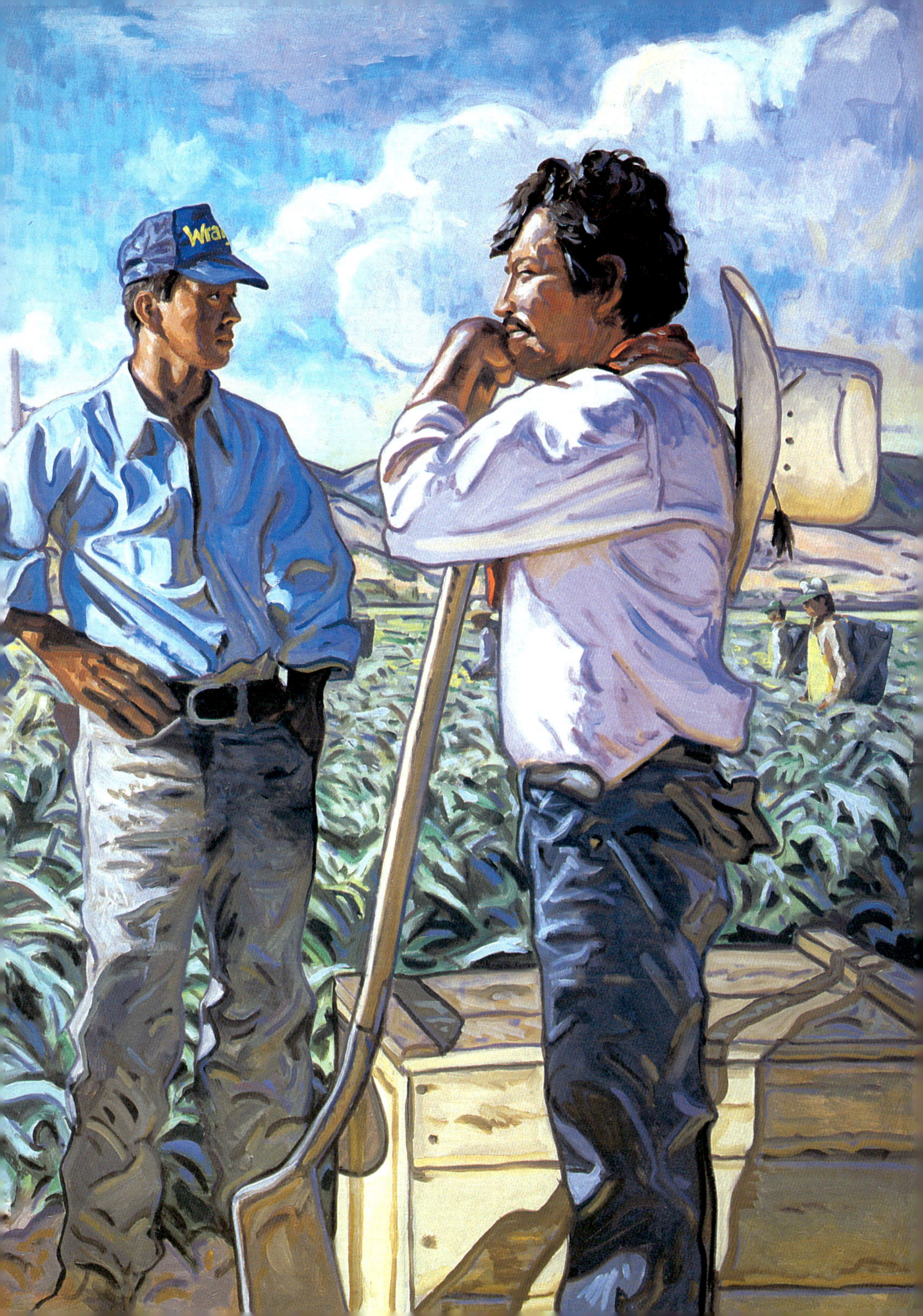
Wra

Buckeye Blake knows that the West can be fun and he delights in variations on the old stereotypes of the past, but the West is also a very real and special place. In the West that Buckeye Blake faces, the hard land calls forth strong qualities from the individual—hard work, a love of nature and of the animals who inhabit it. It also calls forth strength from the artist, reworking ideas, drawing upon the past, yet utilizing media and subjects appropriate for the 20th-century West.

A final comparison with Charles M. Russell finds Blake similar to his predecessor in the variety of styles and approaches he takes in his art, using one stylistic vocabulary for his humorous works, a somewhat different idiom for his more serious subjects. Yet it is through this choosing of styles that Blake has developed as an artist, experimenting with different media, working out patterns of lines and shapes. With his identity as a westerner quite firm, Blake underlines the *art* in cowboy art through his investigations of style.

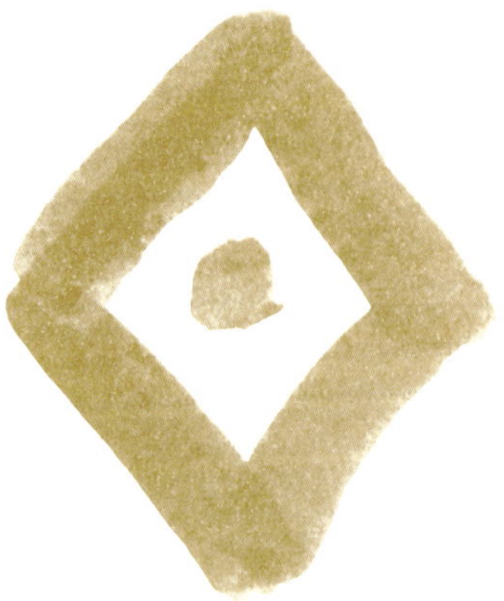

Organized by the Buffalo Bill Historical Center, the exhibition *Buckeye Blake: Art on the Western Front* was funded in part by a generous donation from Mr. Dan Lufkin. The exhibition catalogue, poster and invitation are sponsored by The Greenwich Workshop, Inc., Trumbull, Connecticut, and Big Horn Gallery, Cody, Wyoming.

Back Cover:
Stool (detail), 1993.
Wood and embossed leather;
24 1/2 x 17 x 17 inches.
Loan from Due-West Furniture,
Rindge, New Hampshire.

Buckeye Blake, 1993.
Photograph by Tona Freeman Blake

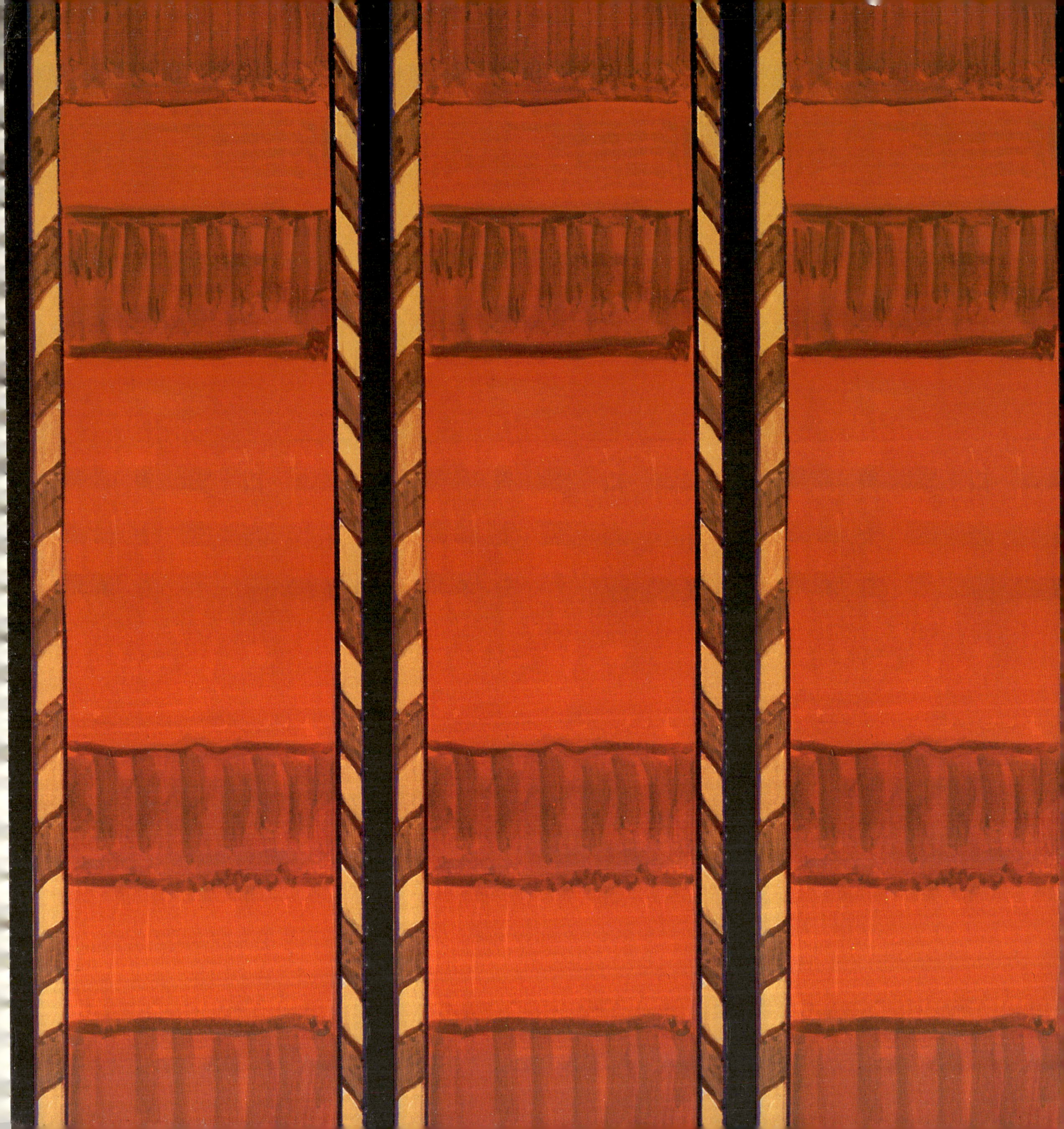